I0539652

GREATER SUM

Greater Sum
Walla Walla, Washington
www.agreatersum.com
facebook.com/GreaterSumJournal

Greater Sum, Issue No. 1, Spring 2017
Copyright © 2017
All Rights Reserved

Cover art: Leonardo da Vinci, *Superficial anatomy of the shoulder and neck (recto)*, pen and ink with wash on paper, 11 ½" x 7 ¾"
Back cover art: Leonardo da Vinci, *Rhombicuboctahedron*
Cover and interior design: Andrew Marcus Corder

Greater Sum is published twice yearly. Subscription rates are $13 for one year (two issues), $25 for two years (four issues); a single copy is $7. Submissions are reviewed year-round; see website (www.agreatersum.com) for submission guidelines.

No part of this work may be reproduced or transmitted in any form or by any means, electronic or mechanical, photocopying, recording, or by any information retrieval or storage system without express written permission except in the case of short excerpts used in critical review.

ISBN: 978-0-9986770-0-2

Printed in the United States of America

GREATER SUM

prose + faith

issue 01, spring 2017

Contents

Tommy and Me

-1-

TOMMY AND I used to bathe together. He was the only child of my parents' best friends, Richard and Sarah. I don't remember much except for the hot soapy smell, the one-eyed Gumby toy, and Tommy's pink bottom when he stood to towel off. I mostly take showers now, just like Tommy. But of course I take mine alone. I grew up to become a real estate agent. He murdered girls until he finally got caught. We've always kept up with each other's careers, albeit from a safe distance.

-2-

Dating is peculiar. It feels like charades and I'm more of a crossword puzzle girl. I think romance is supposed to be more like poetry. If so, my dates are the kind with obvious rhyme lines, troublesome meter, and no real point. And I always catch myself laughing in the wrong places. Most guys are threatened by random laughter from pretty girls. I think I remember Tommy laughing a lot, though I can't quite picture it now.

-3-

I modeled for a while in Chicago. Not runway stuff; catalogs mostly.

I specialized in winter-wear—drab colors, a lot of wool and boots and caps and scarves. I did one rather inelegant shoot in only a bra. It wasn't sexy; it was for Sears. I was proud enough to keep a few copies, but too embarrassed to ever look at them again. My modeling career ended abruptly when a meth-addled photographer told me to uncross my eyes. I knew he was teasing, maybe flirting, because I'd never been able to cross my eyes before—Tommy tried to teach me when we were nine or so. But once the guy with the camera mentioned it, I couldn't seem to focus on anything but the end of my nose during photo shoots. I did one final sunglasses ad before running out of money and moving back to Kentucky.

-4-

Tommy writes me letters every week. He reminisces a lot, but his memories feel oddly distant to me, familiar but unreliable. It's as if our shared history went through an amicable divorce. Tommy got custody of the tire swing, the skating rink, the snapper turtle with the fingernail-polish T on its back, and the ironic mixtapes. The good memories grew up and naturally favored their father. And to further mix this metaphor, I got the furniture, the cars, the tree fort, the obvious stuff that inevitably fades or crumbles. I always write Tommy back, in part to remember, but mostly to try to fix him. I suspect he's beyond repair, but I can't not try.

-5-

A thousand million years ago I used to wake up in our tree fort to see Tommy propped on one elbow, watching me sleep. I remember his wet eyes, the fake cherry smell on his breath, the red food color-ing on his tongue as he tickled my forearm and tried to coax me back to sleep. Most of the girls Tommy killed looked like me. One victim even appeared to have her eyes crossed in the crime scene

8

photographs. But that detail is apocryphal; it must be. Tommy was already in prison when I finally learned to cross my eyes. He should have kissed me back then. Things would be different now.

-6-

Sometimes I wonder if he killed the girls to make them look like me. Other times I wonder if he was killing me when he wrung the last few breaths from those girls. He said in a letter once it had nothing to do with me, which kind of hurt my feelings. I sleep with the lights on now.

-7-

Tommy says he found Jesus in prison. That image makes me smile—a Last Supper rendering with the son of God doling out communion wafers and grape juice to twelve men in orange jumpsuits, their sandaled feet all shackled together under the table. But then my smile blisters and fades and my eyes do begin to cross because it's just not fair. It's not fair that those girls got to see that side of Tommy, that he coaxed them all to sleep, that God now seems to be smiling at Tommy instead of me. Sometimes I dream that Jesus makes parole and comes looking for me. It's not as funny as it sounds.

-8-

I have to show a quaint English Tudor to the Nelsons at two, a farmhouse to the Tindalls at four-thirty, then find a parking space downtown for a real estate seminar at six. Afterward, I'm supposed to meet a guy named Stephen for drinks. But eventually I'll drive by Richard and Sarah's house on the way home. Their lights will be on too. Tommy's dad will be praying for his murderous son and his mom will be drinking in front of the television. I'll park across the street, sucking on cherry candy and fondling both good eyes of the Gumby toy that hangs from my rearview. But mostly I'll watch and wait for one good Tommy memory. When I find it, I'll take it home and cuddle up next to it and try to sleep with my eyes open. But I won't sleep. I'll get up and write yet another letter. Maybe this time I'll address it to me. Maybe I'll find the courage to tell me what I really think. Maybe. The truth is that I envy Tommy, his ordered existence, his assurance of salvation, his ability to remember the good and go on living in spite of the other.

This Earth Is Blessed

Do Not Play in the Holy Dirt

EVEN THOUGH VISITORS have been eating Santuario de Chimayo's holy dirt for centuries, the church's official statement discourages one from doing so, and suggests instead to think of one's many blessings, say an Our Father or two, and gently rub dirt onto ailing spots.

I had walked three miles on the highway's shoulder to the sanctuary with full intention of eating the soil. Not only did I want to taste the magic dirt, but I also wanted to send a vial to my mother for her to eat or rub on her one, remaining breast, which had a lump and was aching. She had lost the first breast to cancer; she did not want to go through chemotherapy a second time. Even though she was not one for rituals, I hoped that at the very least she might set the dirt on a shelf to permeate the living room with good, healthy vibes.

I wasn't alone in either my trek or my desire. Each year, tens of thousands of people pilgrimage to Chimayo during Holy Week with similar intentions. Most aim to reach the church by Good Friday, where they evoke Christ's passion before his Easter resurrection. Many carry large, wooden crosses on their backs while they walk.

The state transportation department provides porta-potties, orange barricades, and signs that direct "Santuario Walkers" and warn traffic to "Watch for Walkers," as well as trashcans, which by Good Friday overflow with empty water bottles. Along the shoulders of a highway 6,000 feet in elevation, often in groups of two to five, these walkers head to the "Lourdes of America" for the holy dirt.

Guided by the snowcapped Sangre de Cristo Mountains—named for a dying Spanish priest's last words—in the distance, pilgrims travel through Santa Fe and the Native American villages of Pojoaque and Nambé along the way. I parked near an intersection in the vast desert outside of a township whose name I did not know and began walking.

"Almost there," I said to a man lumbering with a huge pack on his back.

"I hope so. I've been walking since Wednesday." Today was Friday. He caught his breath, then said, "From Las Lunas."

If he'd driven, it would have taken him about two hours by car to travel the 112 miles. I met him on the pilgrim path when he had but three miles to go, up a hill and down into the Santa Cruz River valley where the Santuario de Chimayo sits.

I asked for what or whom he was walking.

"Good health to my family," he said.

❉

The entrance to Chimayo is a network of participatory shrines. Handmade crosses have been woven into the chain-link fence. In one corner stood the Virgin; round, smooth stones spilled forth from her feet. Each one had a prayer written on it. *Sr. Protégé a nuestra Fam. Orozco Cd. Juarez, Chih. Bless la familia Cano. Please Lord pray for Domingo Sena. RIP Flora Guerrero.*

Across the way, in a covered alcove, votive candles were mounted alongside photographs of people and their requests for blessings.

The Holy Week-booming tourist industry in town sold all things religious: rosaries, vials of collected dirt, bottles of holy water, hand-carved saint figurines, crosses, and Virgin of Guadalupe T-shirts, baseball caps, and necklaces. Outside of a restaurant, a painted image of Jesus juxtaposed against a sign that read, "Eat More Chile." I stopped for a piña colada *paleta*, a homemade pineapple-coconut popsicle with a frozen cherry in the center, before continuing on to the main chapel. The line to enter the chapel snaked across the plaza and wrapped up a dirt road. Most of the pilgrims wore T-shirts and jeans, not the Sunday best I'd grown accustomed to on Easter weekends. Families bulged in the line, and small groups of children left to get paletas or play in the plaza.

The small chapel had that sensual adobe look that a building can have only when the mud stucco has been healed over the brick by hand. Against the building leaned walking sticks and crosses six feet tall, borne here by the devout. A man with a ponytail, wearing a sleeveless shirt, carried a mop bucket out of the church. On the plastic bucket, someone had written in Sharpie, "Holy Water ONLY." He refilled at a small cistern. People cut out of line to fill their empty bottles with the cool, blessed water.

❂

Inside the church, a tall Jesus stood, carved out of a cottonwood tree. His hands and feet were overly large, which added to his folk-art feel. Behind the altar, tucked in his *reredos*, a lanced-and-wounded Jesus looked down on his flock in forgiveness.

I was more interested in the left exit, which led to the *pósito*. This "little dirt well" was about eighteen inches wide and nine inches deep. While rumors suggest divine intervention refills the hole, a competing rumor says that it's trucked in from the local hills. Priests store the dirt in five-gallon buckets and add to the pósito each night.

A sign on the wall read: "Do Not Play in the Holy Dirt." Two small spades and a trowel—neon plastic beach toys—invited the pilgrims to collect dirt. People crowded the hole, filling vials and ziplock baggies. One father rubbed sand over his son and said a prayer. When it came my turn, I kneeled down and filled my two small vials.

❂

In the early 1900s, John Peabody Harrington wrote that the Tewa Native Americans knew Chimayo as a healing spot, *Tsimajo*, where a muddy pool had certain mystical properties. The sacred place's first Hispanic settlement, Plaza del Cerro, was established by the 1740s. As a plaza enclosed by adobe buildings, it was split by the Acequia Madre, the main irrigation channel feeding small gardens of chiles, corn, and beans, and a few wild plum trees.

The legend of the Santuario itself has a few variations.

In one story, a priest came to town only to find the townsfolk unmoved by his requests for a chapel. He bade for a chapel and the people shrugged their shoulders, until one day he disappeared. His requests must have been persistent enough that the people went looking for him, and they found what was presumed to be his body the following day. On the spot he demarcated for the chapel, where there was once a cleared spot of land, a cottonwood tree now grew. The tree's sudden appearance was not as remarkable as its most striking feature: a foot stuck out of the tangle of roots. The townsfolk were sufficiently impressed by this miracle and built his chapel.

The most famous story, however, centers on a trader named Don Bernardo Abeyta, who was gravely ill. Sometimes he is referred to as a shepherd walking the hills with his sheep when he saw a bright, pure light shining out of a spot in the ground. He began digging in the sunny sand, and there found a crucifix. The dirt well he dug and the crucifix healed him, either at that moment or later in life, depending on the tale. He took the cross to the local priest, who organized a procession to relocate it to a chapel in the nearby town of Santa Cruz, where it would be housed. During the night, the crucifix disappeared. Abeyta found it again in the dirt well, and again they carried it to

Santa Cruz, and again it disappeared only to be found in the hole. After this story repeated a third time, the people realized that the crucifix wanted to stay put by the pósito; there they erected the chapel.

This crucifix, hanging in the nave, has an image related to the Black Christ of Esquipulas, Guatemala. The Black Christ, or "Our Lord of Esquipulas," has an interesting history of its own. The original was carved of balsam and orangewood in the late 1500s, and due to the smoke from incense in his church, the dark wood turned darker still. He began to represent a syncretism of religions and place, an image reflecting the dark skin color of the locals. Already positioned on the pilgrimage route to Copán, *el Cristo Negro* in Esquipulas quickly became a destination in his own right. Pilgrims visiting the area claimed to have been healed of everything from leprosy to insanity, blindness to tetanus, yellow fever to hemorrhages. One of the devotions sold there is *tierra santa*, white clay tablets stamped with images of Our Lord of Esquipulas. Eaten or dissolved in water and drunk, these *benditos* seem to heal almost any ailment. By the end of the 1700s, the cult had spread to forty towns in Central America, including Veracruz, Chiapas, and Guadalajara in Mexico. Perhaps the practice of eating sacred earth followed el Cristo Negro north all the way to Chimayo.

☼

The magic dirt of Chimayo was a sandy loam that crumbled and sifted through my fingers; in it was a mixture of Precambrian granite, mica, quartz, and shale. One might also find a few broken roots from mountain muhly, a bit of piñon bark, Arizona fescue, or dried blue grama stems—evidence that the blessed earth comes not from a magically refilling pósito but from the back slopes of surrounding escarpments.

While kneeling at the pósito, I sampled some dirt. It was not the first time I'd eaten earth and the taste was indistinguishable from my memories of what dirt was like in my mouth. It's not that I expected a flavor, but maybe a feeling. What would a divine sensation feel like? It did not feel holy, but gritty.

Later, I looked up why the dirt may be healing. One source suggested that carbonates in the soil might produce the same kind of effervescence that heals heartburn by neutralizing acidity, just as baking soda does. It could have similar amounts of minerals one might find in an industrially processed multivitamin: calcium, copper, manganese, potassium, zinc, cobalt, iron, and selenium.

These properties, however, could not account for all of the miracles attributed to the dirt. Crutches lined one wall of the anteroom exiting the pósito. I doubt anyone had walked three days on crutches due to a severe case of heartburn, or that a one-a-day vitamin could help one shed a leg brace.

Before I came here, I had asked a friend in a wheelchair if she'd ever been to Santuario de Chimayo. "No," she said. "Too much expectation." With her hand, she indicated her motorized wheelchair would have to be left at the chapel.

☀

When I returned home, I mixed the holy dirt with Epsom salts to heal my blistered feet. Perhaps because I did not say any Our Fathers, or am not Catholic, the magic did not work. My blisters were likely nothing compared to those on the feet of the man walking from Las Lunas, walking for the health of his family; my aches surely paled in comparison to those of the pilgrims who lugged heavy wooden crosses down the desert highways—and yet these were the faithful who would return each year in search of holy earth. The blisters did not go away, and although I did not really expect them to, part of me wondered if the results would be different if I'd eaten it instead. I knew it was silly to think that ingesting desert earth could heal anything, from blisters to breast cancer, but that's what faith does—it sifts through any cracks of uncertainty.

Even though I was doubtful, I prepared the second vial to send to my mother. The vial had a small, shiny sticker of Santo Niño de Atocha on it. Even he was barefoot. I wanted a belief, hope that her lump would disappear if she rubbed the dirt on it. I folded bubble wrap around the vial and sealed it in a padded envelope. By her name and address, I wrote, "Fragile." Then I walked it over to the post office. The sun was setting, this time with neon pink clouds and lightning promising a drizzle of rain someplace far, far away.

Drawn from the Water

THE CRUNCH OF the enforcer's boots in the sand sent a shiver down Lexi's spine despite the desert heat beating down on her. She slid behind the fat palm she'd just finished stripping of all the fruit it had to offer. With her back pressed painfully into the protruding bark, Lexi risked a glance around the edge of the tree. A blinding white suit and helmet were headed away from her with a hand resting casually on a holstered phaser. Lexi released the breath she'd been holding as the man slowly disappeared through the rows of date palms laid out in front of her.

"Cynsi, report," Lexi said.

The android's head snapped up at the sound of her name, accompanied by the harsh scraping of sand between her titanium plating. Lexi cringed at the familiar sound. It was something she would never get used to.

"Eighteen hundred hours. One hundred and twelve degrees Fahrenheit. Estimated productivity: low to average. Approximately nineteen pounds of dates collected. Your service is appreciated, nuli worker." Cynsi's monotonous voice was almost lost on the hot wind that whipped hair around Lexi's face and sand around her ankles.

Lexi wrinkled her nose at Cynsi's familiar words: nuli worker. Slave laborer.

"I'm sure it is. Cynsi, assist."

Bending down on one knee, Cynsi lifted the heavy leather cord over her shoulder. The cord pulled tight against a full basket of dates.

As the android got to her feet, Lexi watched the waves of heat dancing over her metal back.

"Get those to the storeroom. I'll see you tomorrow, Cynsi." Wending her way through the palms, Lexi did her best to catch every bit of shade possible beneath the squat trees. She stalled when she reached the tree line, remembering her mother's craving that morning for date pudding. Reaching up to the lowest hanging cluster of dates, she held tight to either side of the white linen curtain hanging around each protruding batch, protecting the fruit from birds. Her tired arms shook the dates as best they could after a full day of working in the desert heat. Kneeling, Lexi found only ten blackened dates spotting the sand at her feet—hardly enough to make pudding. She shoved them quickly into her pockets and set off for her domicile.

Distributed evenly around the perimeter of the date field stood numerous glassy, black poles, vertically striped with silver lights. Between the poles stretched a hazy, iridescent force field. Lexi held her arms out to her sides, palms facing down, and the force field dimmed as she passed through, registering her identity.

"Hey, kid. Why didn't you wait for me?"

Lexi turned sharply to her left where her older brother, Ben, walked coolly, as though he hadn't been working under the same three suns she had for the last ten hours. "Oh. I'm sorry. The suns are frying my brain."

"Something is always frying your brain, kid. Last week it was the light from the cycomp. Today it's the suns. Maybe in ten years you'll be able to blame it on the baby, like Mom." He winked, and Lexi rolled her eyes.

"You probably shouldn't be talking about that out here. Someone might hear you." She glanced over her shoulder, half expecting an enforcer to jump out of the bushes and arrest them. Instead, she saw only droves of workers streaming out of the date fields, bent-backed and glassy-eyed. The nearest enforcers stood atop the glass watchtower that displayed the time in bright green numbers along the side. The glare from the glass caught Lexi in the face, and she turned away, eyes watering.

"Don't be so paranoid." Ben slung one arm over her shoulders and squeezed. "Who ever said a little bit like you could worry about stuff like that anyway? Mom and Dad have it under control, Lex. Only a couple more weeks and things can go back to normal. Well . . . sorta." Ben's brow furrowed. Clearing his throat, he held out a handful of dates. "Hey, want one?"

Lexi's stomach churned at the sight of the dates. "Normal? This is normal now, Ben! Do you *want* to get caught? We're going to get away with this. I know it." She tried to ignore the look of pity on Ben's face. This had to work. She couldn't imagine how her mother would react if someone found out and reported them.

As they trudged slowly uphill, Lexi looked down at her feet, trying to concentrate only on putting one foot in front of the other. Cresting the top of the hill, her heart lightened at the sight of hundreds of rows of tiny, gray domiciles against the pale red of the sand. Behind the last row of homes towered the Xiran Mountains. In the receding light, Lexi could just make out a silvery glow radiating from between its many ragged slopes. Waves of heat covered the valley below in the presence of the rapidly sinking suns. The whole sky turned bright orange as they reached the bottom of the hill, and the brother and sister stopped walking to take in the sunset.

After a moment of silence, Ben plucked at Lexi's sleeve. "Come on, kid. They're waiting for us." He popped a date into his mouth and spit the seed into the sand.

Lexi grabbed the rest of the dates out of his hand. "Don't eat those. I need a few more to make Mom some pudding."

His hand stayed outstretched as he took in the loss of his snack. Then, letting his arm fall to his side, he shrugged. "Fine. I wouldn't mind it in pudding form, I guess."

They were passing through the three-foot gap between the cube-shaped domiciles when Lexi felt fingers wrap tightly around her bicep and yank her down into the sand. "Ouch! Be—" Ben's dusty hand came up and covered her lips. She could taste salt and sweat before she had time to shut her mouth. Shoving his hand away, she glared at her brother, now crouching down beside her. "Gross!" Lexi whispered. "My mouth was open!"

"Shut up and look over there," he hissed into her ear. She followed his pointing finger through the gap between the domiciles and across the narrow street. Through a slow stream of workers returning home, Lexi could see the black number 4003 stamped across the front door of one of the domiciles. Only fifteen doors down from their own. The small gray residence had the same iridescent silver window coverings as every other home in the valley, used only during the harsh summer months to reflect the heat.

"I don't see anything."

Ben grasped her arm again, pulling her in front of him so that her face was pressed up against the wall. From her new vantage point, Lexi could just make out the front end of a sleek white sand rover. An enforcer's sand rover.

Crouching low to the ground, Ben inched his way forward with Lexi in his wake. A few more feet afforded them a view of the rover's left side hatch, which opened with a loud gush of hydraulic steam. A broad-shouldered enforcer stepped out in a pristine white uniform, his helmet's silver visor reaching almost to his chest. Its sharp, reflective surface caught the receding light and sent it skittering across the surface of the domicile he was parked next to.

Following just behind was a federal midwife carrying a small steel case. A silver strip of glass about one inch thick stretched from ear to ear over her eyes, and Lexi wondered what it was for.

They made their way to the front door and knocked only twice. "Close." The enforcer's voice came out equally as bored as the midwife's face looked. The command was apparently meant for the rover's hatch since a moment later it began to descend. A loud click reverberated through the street as the door closed and locked.

The heavy steel door of the domicile slid back, and a loud scraping of sand between metal sent a shiver down Lexi's arms. She could hear a man's trembling voice greeting the officials and the sound of the door sliding shut, but Lexi couldn't tear her eyes away from the locked hatch of the rover. She had seen one like this only once before, but that had been enough to cement its image in her memory forever. Instead of the traditional enforcer's symbol, emblazoned on the side of the rover was the silhouette of a pregnant woman sitting cross-legged, her arms cradling her protruding belly. Printed on the woman's stomach with red paint-like strokes was the female gender symbol. It was elegant in its simplicity, and yet, at the sight of this emblem, Lexi had to press her palm flat against the wall to keep herself upright.

A feminine cry rent the air, followed by stuttered sobbing. Soon a man's incoherent pleading joined in, then a toddler's whimpering cry. Lexi put her hands flat over both ears, bent forward, and placed her head between her knees to block out the sound. Still the sobbing managed to slip between the cracks of her fingers and assail her for what felt like an eternity. Paralyzed with fear that the enforcer would return at any moment, Lexi wasn't able to move from her crouched position in the narrow passageway.

"Lex. Lexi!" Ben was shaking her by the shoulders, but she couldn't bring herself to look up. "Lexi, they're gone. We need to go. Mom's gonna be worried."

Lifting her head an infinitesimal amount, Lexi peered up at the place the sand rover had sat only minutes before. The dust from its treads had already settled. She let Ben help her to her feet and pull her toward the street where a chorus of sobbing could still be heard leaking from number 4003. They padded through the loose dust in the rover's tracks and past the door that had admitted the enforcer and midwife.

The sand seemed to swirl at Lexi's feet as they made their way home, even though the air was perfectly still. Only feet away from their own door, Lexi stopped and grabbed Ben's wrist. "Is that what you mean by *normal*?"

"Of course not, Lex! That isn't going to happen to us. Mom and Dad won't let it happen." His face was stern, and his jaw was clenched. Lexi couldn't read his expression.

"What do you mean? You're hiding something from me, aren't you? What are they going to do?" Lexi could hear her voice becoming hysterical, and she didn't try to stop it.

"Shut up, Lexi! Get inside if you wanna throw a fit. This is why they didn't want to tell you sooner." Ben brushed past her and shoved his fist into the sensor.

"Identity unknown," said a chipper feminine voice. "Please place your thumb and forefinger firmly against the sensor. Identity recognized. Domicile access granted. Have a pleasant day, nuli worker."

Lexi rushed into the one-room dwelling to find her mom standing by the sink with one hand cradling her baby brother against her chest. She was barefoot and clothed in a loose-fitting linen dress that hid her postpartum figure well. Pulling a black braid over her shoulder, she turned to face them with a sleepy smile on her mouth. "Hey, you two." Her smile slipped away as she took in the looks on her children's faces. "What's wrong?"

Lexi worked to control her breathing, but she still couldn't get the words out. From behind her, Ben released an exasperated sigh. "You'd better tell her the plan now. She's freaking out because someone reported 4003's baby. An enforcer just showed up and took him away a few minutes ago. We saw the whole thing. Or heard the whole thing, I mean."

Despite his sardonic tone, Ben's eyes were full of sympathy when he looked over at his little sister. As much as she drove him crazy, Lexi knew he hated that she had seen what happened to that family.

Their mother's face became ashen as her son's words washed over her. She didn't speak as she walked gently across the room and eased the sleeping infant onto her bed where a swaddle was already

24

laid out. He gave only one soft cry as she crossed the corners of the fabric deftly over his still-sleeping form. Next to the bed sat a makeshift bassinet: a pulley bucket from the lagulinth mines in the Xiran Mountains—the planet's main source of fuel and energy. Their father had fashioned it from an old chained elevator bucket as soon as their mother announced her pregnancy. He knew no one would ever miss the shallow basin since the mines no longer used any sort of pulley system.

At the time, no one had questioned him when he brought it home. It was common knowledge in the valley that the nuli workers would only be provided with newborn supplies if the pregnancy had been reported and the carry had been approved by the emperor's court. So they were never reported. The workers were forced to provide their own inferior midwifery and disguise their weight gain for as long as possible. The latter half of their pregnancy would become completely dependent on a decades-old rumor about the worker women being particularly susceptible to Tanovar's disease—or sun poisoning. Women were often bedridden for months on end, as the disease was known to affect them more severely.

It was a convenient cover story, yet it could only last so long. They may have been excused from work for many months, but never years. Often the nuli families would pass their baby boys around the valley to different women as they went on leave from the field—something that normally resulted in the child being seen by an enforcer.

After laying the baby between two rolled-up kitchen towels in the bassinet, she turned around to face them, face still very pale. "What happened?"

Ben immediately started in on what they'd seen down the street, and Lexi made her way over to the bassinet, not caring to relive the scene again. Perching herself on the edge of her parents' bed, she peered down into the bassinet. Her baby brother's eyes roved beneath closed lids, and Lexi knew he was dreaming. Lips parting, his mouth formed a small *O* that widened and contracted slightly but never closed. Kneeling down beside him, she stroked his impossibly soft cheek with the back of her finger. His cinnamon-tinted skin felt tissue thin beneath the press of her hand. She wondered how she could love anyone as much as she loved him. Somehow it didn't seem possible that she would love even her own children any more.

Lexi's thoughts were interrupted by the harsh scraping of sand between metal, and her hand tightened into a fist instinctively at the sound. She didn't have to look up to know her father was home from work. Ben had just finished speaking when the *clomp clomp* of heavy boots was heard coming over the dusty threshold. Lexi glanced up at her mother's face and was surprised to find her looking saddened but somewhat relieved. The doors scraped shut, and a dull *thunk* from the corner told her that her father had removed his boots. She still didn't look over at him, knowing he would soon ask what they were talking about and Ben would have to tell the story all over again.

As if on cue, her father's gruff voice barked down at his son, "What's goin' on, boy? Looks like you've had a time of it."

Lexi prepared to block out the sound of Ben's voice again, but instead she found herself straining to hear what her mother whispered to her father. ". . . overheard some commotion after work. They terminated 4003's pregnancy, Samuel. I guess it was a boy after all. I thought she looked like she was carrying high. Poor thing."

Her father grunted his agreement. "Not gonna affect us, I'd guess. She weren't very far along anyhow. Still leavin' the domicile some-times. Coulda been an enforcer that saw she was carryin'. Give it a bit more time, Laria."

At this, Lexi's head snapped up in time to see her father's massive hand gently squeeze her mother's shoulder. His face was coated in more silvery lagulinth dust than usual.

"What does that mean? What are you giving more time?" Lexi's voice warbled slightly, and she gripped the sides of the bassinet.

He turned his face toward Lexi, and she noticed glistening clumps of silver dust stuck to his temples where sweat dripped from his hairline. A look of regret flitted across his features, replaced by one of resolve. Without a word, he crossed toward her, leaving a light dusting of silver in his wake. He shooed her away from his bed, and she understood he meant to change out of his dirty clothes.

Crossing the room, Lexi located the date pitter in the sink and gave it a quick rinse before starting on her meager pile of fruit. After pitting a few of the dates, she glanced over at her mother to see if she was planning on answering her questions or simply ignoring them. Standing unusually straight-backed, Laria's eyes stared at nothing in particular, her fingers worrying her bottom lip.

Lexi went back to the dates until she had them all pitted and chopped. Rapping the screen above the sink with her knuckles, she called, "Allenius." The screen brightened. "To start, one and a half cups of flour please."

"Insufficient supply," a pleasant male voice responded.

"Well, then three quarters cup." A frail metal tray extended out of the wall just to the left of the kitchen sink, coated in a thin layer of sand. When Lexi lifted the small bowl of flour from its perch, she could see traces of the red dust mixed in. "Yuck," she murmured to herself.

From behind her, she heard an annoyed sigh and someone's hand slap a knee. She turned to find the rest of her family having a silent argument, complete with wild gesturing and an eye roll from Ben.

"Here's what I already know," Lexi said loudly from the kitchen. Everyone stopped talking, and three surprised faces turned in her direction. "I know that they ended that woman's pregnancy today because her baby was the wrong gender. I know that we'll get in a lot of trouble if the enforcers find our baby. What I don't know is what you're planning on doing about it. Why did you tell Ben and not me? I love him just as much as Ben does. Probably more. I can help if you tell me what's going on. Please." She tried to keep the whine out of her voice, but it came through anyway.

"Come here, kid." Samuel waved her over to the bed, gesturing

27

for her to sit down. "It's got nothin' to do with who loves who more. We know you love your brother." He sighed and wiped his hand down his face. He looked completely exhausted, and a twinge of guilt hit Lexi for forcing a confession from her parents.

After looking her over for a minute, her father shook his head and stood up from the bed. "We're not talkin' about it anymore right now. I want you to actually sleep tonight, Lex. We'll talk in the morning, and you can think about it all you want tomorrow. Finish whatever you're makin' and we'll get to bed early." There was a note of finality in his voice that told Lexi it wouldn't do any good to argue.

Regretfully, Lexi rose, fingernails leaving crescent shapes in the palms of both hands. She joined her mother in the kitchen as Laria prepared their evening meal. Lexi's mind wasn't kind to her as she mechanically stirred and poured the pudding. Daydreams and visions of a passing enforcer hearing a baby's cry and breaking down the door assaulted her as she baked.

Halfway through, the infant woke up and needed to nurse, leaving dinner preparations forgotten. Lexi finished dinner too while imagining the lifeless form of her baby brother being carried away by the bored-looking midwife.

Leaving her father and older brother to eat, Lexi went to sit at her mother's feet while Laria burped the baby. "Why do they hate us, Mom?"

"Hate us? I've never thought about it quite like that. I guess they do. But mostly they're just afraid of us." The rhythmic sound of her hand against the baby's back stopped, and she pulled Lexi's hair over her shoulder, rubbing the back of her hand over her daughter's neck.

"Afraid of us? But don't they know that we're afraid of them?" Lexi leaned her head forward slightly as Laria continued to use her free hand to massage Lexi's neck.

"I suppose they do know that, yes. They must or they would never have enslaved us. But they have reason to be afraid. We outnumber them three to one at least. If we rose up against them, there's a good chance we might win the fight. That's why they started to take our boys from us two years ago. They think that without men, our numbers will eventually decrease."

From the other side of the room came a resounding *thump*. Straightening, Lexi looked over toward her older brother and father who sat in the corner with their bowls in their laps. Flipping over the heavy work boot, Samuel exposed the gray sludge of a smashed narlar beetle. "Insects. That's what they think of us. Numerous and stupid. What do they care if they're murderin' our kids right in front of our eyes? But we're resilient. Kill one of us an' two more'll take his place."

Knock knock knock. Lexi stirred and pressed her face deeper into her pillow. She didn't feel like it was time to get up for work quite yet. Why would someone knock on their door this early in the morning?

She heard her father's feet hit the floor and shuffle toward the door. Lexi turned onto her side in time to see her mother snatch the bucket part of the bassinet off its holder. Walking quickly across the room, she lowered the sleeping baby, bucket and all, into a large date basket that had been sitting empty on the kitchen floor for the last few weeks.

Samuel watched from across the room, waiting for Laria to return to bed and stash the remaining evidence of their crime—the legs of the bassinet and a couple of tiny blankets—before opening the door. As soon as the loud grinding of the door halted, an anxious panting sound filled the domicile. Lexi pushed herself onto her elbows and tried to peer around the doorframe.

A young man with shoulder-length brown hair and no shoes stood outside with one hand propped against the side of the house, trying to catch his breath. She recognized him as a neighbor from the street behind theirs, but she couldn't remember his name.

"Jules . . . heard about . . . the baby." He cleared his throat and took a few deep breaths while Laria crossed the room to stand next to her husband. "I overheard him say he's gonna report you. You've gotta get rid of it. Now!"

Even in the pale light of early morning coming through the open door, Lexi could see her mother's face lose all its beautiful honeyed color. She clutched at Samuel's arm, and her husband caught hold of her waist to hold her firmly upright.

The young man leaned in closer. "You've got to hurry. The enforcers start rounds just after sunrise. If you're on their list, they could be here within the hour. May the God of All Realms be with you." He left with a tight nod.

Before the door had shut all the way, Samuel was already barking orders at his family. "Ben, get dressed. Pack food for your mom and sister. Laria, nurse him now while you can. An hour was probably too generous. Lexi, put on your red tunic. You're gonna need to blend in." He crossed to the basket that held the pulley bucket and began arranging kitchen towels and scraps of old clothing around it.

Lexi was up and dressed in time to help her father secure the baby's bed. It was an older basket and unusually blackened on the inside with smashed and dried dates. It had obviously been stolen from the date fields, and she wondered how her father had managed to take it. He didn't even work in the fields.

"Dad, where did this thing come from anyway?"

"Had a friend steal it from the storeroom." He didn't look up at her as he finished arranging the bucket to fit snugly in the bottom of the basket. Even with all the extra padding, there was still a good ten inches of space above the rim of the bucket.

Laria bent down between them and lowered her milk-drunk baby boy into his bed. He stared up at them, eyes only half open, and the corners of his mouth seemed to turn up in the tiniest of smiles. Lexi's heart hammered as she hovered over him, still in the dark about her parents' plan for their youngest child. Did it even matter anymore? How had this morning's events changed things?

"You need to go now before the first sun is up." Samuel bent and threw the leather strap over Laria's shoulder. "Can you manage it?"

Opening her mouth to respond, the words caught in Laria's mouth and tears sprang to her eyes. She cleared her throat and nodded.

"Where are we going?" Lexi asked. But no one responded. Lexi felt Ben come up behind her and throw a small satchel across her shoulders. She looked down to see a brown leather bag filled with the food he'd been instructed to gather. Ben's hands came up to rest on her shoulders, and he turned her around to face him.

"Take care of my brother, kid. I'll make up some excuse for you today. Not sure what yet, but no doubt it'll be brilliant." He winked, trying to look confident but failing.

Before Lexi was able to respond, her mother's hand slipped into her own and pulled her toward the door. It ground open to let them pass through, and Lexi glanced back at her father. His eyes looked at them sharply and his lips were set into a thin line.

"It's gonna be okay, Daddy," Lexi lied. His eyes softened slightly, and the door slid shut between them. Laria was already waiting in the shadows between the domiciles in front of theirs. She beckoned for Lexi to hurry up.

"What are we going to do with him, Mom?"

"Shh. Not now. We need to reach the fields," Laria whispered over her shoulder as they made their way through the narrow passage. In the dim light between the homes, her mother's silhouette looked hunchbacked as she slogged through the sand, the basket swaying with every step.

Lexi concentrated on the sound of the wind passing through the narrow streets and slipping between the buildings. It soothed her to hear nothing but the breeze and the *pad pad pad* of their footsteps on the red sand.

They had passed through four rows of domiciles without yet

seeing a single person leaving for work. Five more streets to go. Lexi's heart beat faster the closer they walked toward the edge of the nuli township. For the moment, the domiciles offered them protection and cover from the coming sand rovers. Once they broke free of the quiet streets, they would be visible to any enforcer descending into their valley.

Two more streets. Lexi glanced down at her red tunic. It was surprisingly close to the color of the sand beneath her feet, worn and dusty from two years of wear and hard labor in the date fields. This was her one consolation as they neared the open desert beyond the gray houses. At least *she* would not draw attention to their little party.

She mouthed a prayer to the God of All Realms that any enforcer they might pass would not care that they were carrying a heavy date basket so close to the township—that they would not be taken for thieves of the emperor's precious resources. One more street, and then the hike uphill toward the fields. Safety awaited them there.

They were a few short yards from breaking free of the domiciles when Lexi saw Laria slide to the ground, her left side pressed against the gray wall. Kneeling down beside the basket where her baby brother still slept, Lexi stared out at what little of the desert she could see through the gap. The breeze picked up, and the sand swirled in its familiar rhythm, creating perfectly spaced patterns and ripples across the empty terrain.

She looked over at her mother for some explanation for the delay and found her eyes turned up and her brow knit in concentration. Laria's eyes met her daughter's and her fingers tapped her ear. Lexi listened hard and was finally able to distinguish the soft thrum of an engine adding its voice to the cadence of the morning's wind.

Plastered against the wall, Lexi didn't seem able to move her arms or legs. And from the look on her mother's face, she was equally terrified. The thrumming grew suddenly louder until it filled the street they'd just come through and probably woke anyone who was still sleeping in the nearby homes. The sand rover slowed to a crawl past the gap they were hiding in and finally stopped where they could just see the tail end of the vehicle.

The baby gave a grunt. Peering down into the basket, they could see him begin to squirm in the confinement of his swaddle. Although his eyes remained closed, he let loose an angry cry. Laria scooped him up before he had reason to complain further. The loud gush of steam from the hatch met Lexi's ears. They would be getting out of the rover now.

The crunch of heavy boots on sand could be heard from the street behind them. Indistinct voices drifted between the domiciles, a cheerful banter between a man and woman. Lexi crept slowly toward the rover and knelt where she could easily see into the street. She couldn't tell if the pair that stood beside the white rover were the same two she'd seen before. All the masters looked the same to her.

The door closed with a snap, and the enforcer leaned against the side of the rover, arms crossed over his chest. The midwife wore the same silver glass over her eyes that Lexi had noticed before. Her hand came up, resting in midair next to her face, and began to flick with one finger as if trying to swat away a tiny insect that Lexi couldn't see.

"Oh god. Are you seeing this? I swear the termination list is at least twice as long as it was six months ago. These women reproduce like rabbits." Her fingers continued to flick at the air next to her eye, and Lexi realized the glass must be some sort of cycomp that she was reading.

The enforcer grunted. "Not exactly the comparison I would have made."

The midwife's hand fell to her side. "Oh, please don't tell me. I don't think I can stomach any of your crass jokes this early in the morning." Her hands went up to rest on her hips, and Lexi saw something silver gleaming on the back of her hand. "You know I don't have a sense of humor until I'm fully awake. Tell me in a couple hours, and I promise I'll laugh."

Lexi moved a few steps closer to the open street to get a look at the mark. She had to crouch down and crane her head to the side to see it clearly, but there was no mistaking the brush strokes of the female gender symbol that caught the light from the rising suns.

The baby, content only temporarily after being picked up, began to fuss and thrash around. Lexi felt helpless as she watched her mother struggle to nurse and calm the restless infant. His hands came loose and flailed against Laria's chest, angry despite the soft cooing coming from his mother's mouth. A tear slipped down Laria's cheek as she continued to fight her baby to attach and nurse.

"What's that sound?" the midwife asked.

Approaching footsteps responded to the inquiry, and Lexi's heart jumped into her throat. She caught her mother's eye and motioned for her to move quickly. Laria ran softly on the balls of her feet between the homes, dragging the basket along behind her with her free hand. Lexi was right on Laria's heels, mere inches from slipping around the corner after her mother when a deep voice rang out behind her.

"Hey! Stop right there!"

Heart hammering, Lexi turned and walked toward the approaching enforcer, hoping to draw attention away from the baby. The crying had stopped, and Lexi silently thanked the God of All Realms. She tried to look merely curious under the enforcer's inspection, although her hands trembled at her sides.

"Where was that crying coming from?" He looked over her shoulder in the direction Laria had just disappeared.

"Yeah, I heard it too! But it seems to have stopped now . . . and I don't see anything. Weird, huh?" Lexi laughed nervously.

The enforcer grunted and shoved her out of the way. Lexi fell hard against the wall and slid to the ground. Helplessly, she watched the man round the corner of the domicile and disappear. Any moment now she would hear her mother's voice yelling in protest. Maybe the baby would start crying again when he was torn from her arms. But nothing happened. The desert was as still as it had been before the arrival of the sand rover.

From the street behind her, Lexi heard two people talking in low voices. A man and a woman. Knees bent, she crept toward the voices and saw that the enforcer was standing next to the rover.

"Oh well. It was probably coming from one of the domiciles anyway," the midwife was saying. Lexi watched as they knocked and entered a domicile.

"Psst!" Lexi looked behind her to see Laria's face peeking around the corner and looking anxious. She backed away slowly, sinking down next to her mother.

"Where did you go?" Lexi asked.

"I hid behind domicile 1278. I'm pretty sure he only checked as far as 1276. Bless the God of All Realms. That was too close."

Back in the basket, the baby's eyes were wide open and taking in the sight of the sky, which they had never seen before. Lexi's lips began to tremble as she stared into his honey-brown eyes. They were going to miss all his firsts. His first steps. His first word. The first time he laughed. Wiping her tear-streaked cheeks on the sleeve of her tunic, Lexi stood and followed after her mother.

It wasn't long before they were safely under the cover of the date palms. Lexi's mind had been reflecting on the conversation she'd overheard and all of the questions she had for her mother. She tried to organize her thoughts and ask only one question at a time.

"Mom, who's Jules?"

"He works with your dad. They don't really get along." Her breathing was ragged, and Lexi could tell that she was tired from carrying the basket.

"Do you want me to carry it for a little while?" Lexi held out her hand, but Laria just shook her head and marched on.

"Why don't they get along?" Lexi could see the little wisps of frustration float across her mother's face. It was too difficult for her to talk when she was spending so much energy hefting the basket over the shifting sand.

"You know Dad got that promotion. He's overseeing the excavation in sector 245 now. Jules thought it should have been him."

Lexi swallowed down the rest of her questions about Jules. "So where are we going, Mom?" Laria stopped and set the basket on the ground. Lexi looked down to meet the curious gaze of her baby brother. His little hint of a smile brought a huge grin to her face.

"There." Lexi looked up and followed the pointing finger. Her eyes landed on the Calderian River through the trees. It was at least another mile away. Her eyes followed the winding river as it traveled west. But the river soon wound its way out of sight around the side of the Jongli Mountains—the range that ran along the western edge of the nuli valley.

"I don't understand." Lexi's brow creased in a deep frown, and she searched her mother's face for an explanation. Instead of responding, Laria lifted the basket and set the strap over her shoulder again. She moved in the direction of the river, Lexi following a few steps behind.

"Do you know where the Calderian River goes?" Laria finally asked as they approached the riverbank.

"Um . . . to Parahitus? Ben's been talking about the city a lot lately. He says he wants to live there someday," she said, rolling her eyes.

"Hm. Well, you're right. It leads to Parahitus." Laria kept walking, and Lexi waited for her mother to say more. But Laria remained silent.

"Mom! We can't—" Lexi began, suddenly realizing what her mother was intending to do. But Laria turned sharply and held her hand up to silence her daughter.

Reaching the bank of the river, they sat and removed their shoes. Lexi inhaled deeply. The musty odor and slight humidity didn't exist anywhere else in the arid desert. Slipping her feet into the cool, green water, the current stripped away the pain from her aching feet in mere seconds.

Lexi sighed and rifled through the satchel Ben had given her that morning. Until that moment, she had forgotten to be hungry. Lifting the food from her bag, she handed off a slice of bread and a few dates to her mother before taking a bite of her own portion.

"This is what we get for letting Ben pack the food," Lexi said with her mouth full of dates. Her throat felt tight, and she had to swallow hard to get the fruit down.

Laria didn't respond as she lifted her baby from his bed and began to nurse him again. This time he didn't fight her and ate greedily. Silent tears ran unchecked down Laria's face as she fed her child. Lexi's throat threatened to close up at the sight of her mother's grief.

They sat there until he had eaten his fill. Then Laria deftly swaddled the infant and placed him in his bassinet. Lexi brushed the bread crumbs from her lap and watched as tears fell from her chin to replace them.

"I need you not to fight me on this, Lexi. Your father and I have already talked about it, and you won't be able to change my mind by begging." Lexi clenched her hands in her lap and didn't say anything. "You know by now that we can't keep him. It's just too dangerous. And giving him to another family in the valley wouldn't be any different. He has to go somewhere else if he's going to have any chance at life, Lex." She placed her hand against her daughter's face and stroked Lexi's cheek with her thumb.

"Say goodbye now, love," Laria whispered.

Lexi ground her teeth together to stop the tirade that reverberated in her mind from escaping through her lips. This wasn't her mother's fault, and she wouldn't take it out on her. A sob burst from Lexi's mouth and caught her off guard. She bent down and brushed a kiss against the tiny forehead, letting herself be as heartbroken as she wanted to be.

"I wish we could keep you," Lexi said, her voice cracking.

Laria stood and began to drag the basket down the riverbank and into the water. Wading out into the current, she let go of her sleeping child. Covering her mouth with both hands, she sobbed as she watched him float lazily away. It was minutes before she was able

37

to return to the shore and sink to the ground beside her daughter. Lexi pulled her knees up to her chest and wrapped her arms tightly around her legs. Her puffy, red eyes looked out at the Calderian River in disbelief.

"This is insane, Mom," she breathed. "I mean it. Completely crazy."

She expected her mother's voice to be broken or for her not to be able to respond at all. Instead the reply she received was full of passion, even anger. "And what else would you suggest we do? The God of All Realms will protect him. It is no longer in our hands. It never was."

Without a word to her mother, Lexi stood and started to walk down the riverbank, keeping the floating basket in her sights. Ducking under low-hanging tree branches and wading through waist-high bushes, she carried her sandals so she could feel the wet sand underfoot.

"Lexi!" Her mother's voice rang out behind her.

"I just have to know if he's okay," Lexi called back over her shoulder.

"Be careful! Don't let them see you!" Laria shouted over the gurgling of the water.

She had no intention of being seen, but she couldn't walk away now either. She had to know what happened to him. Her mother would be able to grieve so much easier knowing her son had been found.

Lexi felt she had walked for at least an hour through thick brambles and soggy fallen trees to keep up with the basket's pace. Sweat dripped from her hairline and into her eyes. She wiped it away hastily and continued her trek through the thinning foliage.

Without warning, Lexi's feet slapped onto a paved road that seared her bare skin, making her jump back into the comfort of the moist sand. Jamming her feet back into her sandals, she jogged for a couple minutes to catch up with her brother's floating bassinet. With only a well manicured row of Xinsia bushes planted evenly along the bank, she was able to easily keep pace with her brother.

In the road to her left, Lexi noticed shining silver specks amongst the black of the pavement. Lagulinth dust, she thought. But what purpose did it serve in the ground? Why would the road need energy? She felt a sudden swell of pride as she realized how dependent the masters were on her father and other men like him. Without them, even their roads would cease to function.

Having finally left the nuli valley behind her, Lexi could clearly see the city of Parahitus nestled in the foothills of the Jongli Mountains. She had never seen anything like it before in her life. Buildings a hundred times bigger than the tiny domiciles in the valley stood close together like crystal leaflets on a palm frond. They were so tall and narrow that Lexi half expected them to topple over right in front of her eyes.

As she walked still closer, she could just make out thousands of flying rovers diving between one another and the impossibly tall buildings. There was a rhythm to their movement, and Lexi found herself caught up in watching their dance, attempting to decode the steps.

Her eyes snagged on what looked like a giant diamond snake suspended even higher above the ground than the rovers were flying. Its many sections allowed it to bend and turn around the sharpest of curves with ease, as if it were really alive. Lexi noticed that it stopped throughout the city at regular intervals.

Her feet began to slow as her eyes hungrily sought out the strange and new sights, devouring each with amusement, confusion, and awe. But there was something niggling at the back of her mind. With a start, Lexi saw the basket floating far ahead. She ran to catch up, her breathing quickly becoming labored.

Once she was walking alongside the basket again, her ears seemed to open for the first time since laying eyes on Parahitus. A soft fussing drifted over the water. How long had he been awake and crying? What was she going to do if he wasn't found soon?

She whispered a prayer that the baby would settle and not start screaming even louder once he realized his mother wouldn't be picking him up. Laria had said that the God of All Realms was in control of her brother's life. It was something her parents had told her and her older brother again and again. Not until this moment had it penetrated Lexi's mind. She repeated her mother's words to herself as she walked beside the Calderian, listening to her brother's continued fussing.

A burst of light feminine laughter floated toward Lexi over the water, and she threw herself beneath the nearest Xinsia bush. Its bright purple flowers and razor-sharp thorns scraped the side of her neck. She pulled back from the bush just far enough to avoid being speared again. Lexi edged closer to the river to find a hole in the leaves to look through.

Three women stood in the water up to their knees talking and laughing together. Two of them had their hair pulled back into tight buns and were in full-length white cotton dresses that they held just above the surface of the water. The third woman was considerably younger and wearing a cobalt-blue dress that hung to mid-thigh. Her long red hair hung down in loose curls, and Lexi's mouth fell open in disbelief. There were a few children in the valley who had yellow hair, but she had never seen red before. Lexi noticed that her skin seemed to be glowing. She squinted, trying to see more clearly, but she was still too far away. Keeping low to the ground, Lexi edged forward. She ducked behind each bush lining the road until she could easily hear their conversation.

The taller woman in white was speaking loudly to her companions, her eyebrows raised and her mouth stretched wide over blindingly white teeth. ". . . was getting another nanite injection last week. I don't care if she *is* a cyborg! She's going to fry what little brains she has left!" Lexi noticed that her eyebrows never moved, giving her a permanent look of surprise.

Her stocky, white-clad friend tittered. "Well, you know I hate to involve myself in anyone's personal affairs, but I just felt that I needed to warn her. If she's not careful, she's going to lose her job and end up as someone's household appliance!"

The woman in blue gave a half-hearted laugh and stared out at the river pensively. Her friends took no notice of her somber attitude and continued to gossip loudly.

"Hush!" the tall woman said suddenly. "Do you hear something?" Lexi watched in suspense as the basket traveled nearer to the women.

The short woman stopped laughing abruptly while her young friend turned to look upriver. Her shining skin reflected the sun, making her appear otherworldly.

"It's—" She walked slowly out into the river, the strength of the current threatening to pull her down. Her eyes widened as they landed on the basket and Lexi pressed a fist into the knot in her stomach. "—a baby crying."

The shorter woman in white looked pityingly at her young companion. "Oh dear, no. You poor thing, hearing babies all the way out—"

"No, Cam! Look!" The redhead pointed a little way downriver where the basket was meandering along. Lexi bit down painfully on her lower lip.

The young woman caught the basket by the leather strap and pulled it out of the current. She bent down over the basket, and her face softened at the sight of the screaming infant. Still standing in the shallows of the river, the two women in white joined their friend. Immediately, the tall woman gasped and reeled back from the basket. She clutched her hands together at her chest and her dress fell into the water.

"Look at the color of its skin! It's a slave child, I just know it. Is it a male?" She seemed not to want to come near the basket again. Lexi nervously shifted her weight from one foot to the other.

The woman in blue didn't share the same repulsion as her friend.

Without hesitation, she lifted the crying baby from his bed and carried him to shore, where two enforcers stood guard. The infant's crying subsided, but he squirmed against her, restless in the unfamiliar embrace.

"Gwenie, drop Raz a cycom. Quickly. Tell him to bring some milk. Be sure it's human in origin." Unwrapping the loosened swaddle, she peeked into the baby's diaper, and Lexi held her breath. Would they kill him when they discovered his gender? But the woman's face betrayed nothing as she cradled the struggling baby awkwardly, attempting to calm him.

Lexi decided that Gwenie must have been the one who had been keeping her distance from the "slave child" because she clicked her tongue and crossed her arms over her chest, refusing to move from her place in the river. Noticing her companion's unwillingness to help, Cam moved quickly out of the water.

"I'm sorry, Your Highness," said Gwenie, not sounding sorry at all, "but if that *is* a male, it should be reported to your father's court and scheduled for execution immediately. We shouldn't be feeding it milk of *any* origin." Despite her use of the term "Highness," Gwenie's voice dripped with condescension and hatred as she watched the baby squirm. With her stomach in knots, Lexi looked to the woman in blue for her reaction.

The younger woman, who Lexi now realized must be some kind of princess, glared at the older woman and stretched to her full height. "His birth family is of no consequence now, Gwen. I'm going to keep him. I hope that in the future, your allegiance to your emperor is strong enough to overcome any former distaste for his new grandson."

Gwenie's face paled, and her wide mouth puckered tightly, making her look as though she'd just swallowed a rotten date. "Highness, he's a *slave*. You can't simply replace a baby of *royal blood* with something you picked up off the street! I know how much you must be hurt—"

"Don't. You know nothing." Her voice was low and dangerous,

her eyes piercing Gwenie with their embittered desperation. "Recall, Gwen, how many inseminations have failed. I know better than anyone that a baby is not merely a house pet to be played with one day and forgotten the next." She returned her attention to the restless infant, crooning over him in a language Lexi didn't recognize.

Holding a small, rectangular black box, Cam returned from where she'd been rummaging through her bag. "Raz." She waited with the box inches from her lips. It beeped softly in reply. "We're in need of infant milk. Make sure it's human. Come quickly." The box beeped twice.

Lexi felt her tunic cinch tightly at the back of her neck, her collar cutting into her throat. Scratching at her neck to release the garment's hold on her, she coughed and sputtered loudly. Whoever was holding her tunic threw her backward toward the ground, her head hitting the lagulinth road with a dull *thunk*. She groaned and rolled off the scorching hot pavement and onto the wet sand. The attacker lifted her prone form up by the shoulders and dropped her face first onto the ground at the princess' feet. Lexi sat up, clumps of sand sticking to the sweat on her face.

"This nuli *trash* was hiding behind that bush, Your Highness. Should I—"

"No. That won't be necessary. Thank you, Hector." The enforcer backed away. Lexi wished she could see the face behind the visor. Did he hate her as much as Gwenie hated Lexi's brother?

But he remained silent, standing perfectly still and communicating none of his personal feelings. Lexi dropped her gaze to the sand.

"Stand up." The princess' voice was neither kind nor cruel. Lexi stood, her eyes growing wide as she looked up at the woman. At such close proximity, her hair was even more beautiful. The red was streaked with various shades of gold and orange that caught the light and glistened like a sunset. Her skin, which Lexi thought had been glowing somehow, was completely covered in intricately drawn silver tattoos.

Lagulinth tattoos, Lexi realized as she gaped openly at the woman.

Tiny vines and delicate flowers sparkled on her face and neck, interwoven with unfamiliar runes and markings. Larger symbols and images seemed to cover the rest of her body but Lexi didn't take the time to examine them. She bowed awkwardly, trying not to fall over.

"Why were you watching us?" the woman demanded.

"I'm sorry. I was following the date basket. I heard a baby crying." That was as close to the truth as she was going to allow herself to get.

"You're a date picker? You don't look old enough." The princess' voice was calm but demanding.

"I'm twelve, Your Highness." Lexi could tell she didn't believe her, but neither did she press the matter. "And I've been a date picker for four years. The Calderian runs right next to the fields. I just followed the basket because I was worried about the baby." It was still only a half-truth. Lexi comforted herself with the thought that she was saving her family from execution by telling that half-truth.

A deep *thwap thwap thwap thwap* came from overhead, and Lexi looked up to see a rover soaring toward them along the lagulinth road. It looked just like a sand rover without the treads. It came to a halt next to their party, hovering a few yards above the road. The side hatch opened and silvery opaque steps spilled down from the rover, causing the lagulinth particles in the pavement below to glisten brightly. Lexi had to look away.

A portly man in a black and white uniform blundered down the stairs carrying a pale yellow cardboard box. Lexi noticed that he had silver tattoos on either side of his neck.

"I'm so sorry, Your Highness. I wasn't able to find the milk you requested. Hard to come by that, you know." He seemed out of breath from his short jog down the rover's stairs. He wiped the back of his hand over his forehead and took a deep breath before continuing.

"This is the best I could find. Will it do, Your Highness?" His brow creased with concern. The young princess took the box from him, reading both the front and back before sighing and dropping it back into his hands.

"Your ignorance is astounding, Raz. Hurry back to the city, and bring me what I need." She looked down at her new baby boy and stroked his cheek. Despite his obvious hunger, the young princess had finally managed to calm the child into a light sleep. Glancing up at Raz, Lexi saw his face grow red. He didn't move to follow the command of his princess.

"I'm s-s-sorry, Your Highness." His blush deepened when she turned her eyes on him. "I truly don't—" Lexi gasped and all eyes turned to rest on her. She covered her mouth with her hands, her face turning nearly as red as Raz.

"Excuse me . . ." Lexi hesitated. "I just thought of a way you could give him milk, Y-Your Highness."

Thwap thwap thwap thwap. Lexi could feel the heavy thrum of the rover's engine through the soles of her sandals as they flew toward the Xiran Mountains. The cockpit window afforded her a full view of the nuli valley where her home was lost in a vast sea of domiciles that stretched as far as the eye could see. A flood of midmorning light made the lagulinth glow from the mountain range imperceptible. Her breath caught at the foreign scene.

Like the waters of the Calderian River, the red sand swirled and pitched around thousands of stalwart domiciles. And yet Lexi knew the domiciles and their occupants could never truly remain steadfast—just as the date basket could never have resisted the pull of the river. Their future rested not with fortune or their own cleverness, but with the same being that directed the flow of the river. The God of All Realms had orchestrated that day's events and protected her brother just as her mother said he would.

The floor seemed to drop out from under Lexi's feet as Raz

abruptly dropped the control wheel. An enforcer—the only other person who was instructed to accompany Lexi home—stood solidly, his feet planted wide.

Lexi clung even tighter to the baby as he kicked and flailed his arms in hunger. They descended rapidly into the midst of the cubed domiciles below. The rover landed directly in front of Lexi's own residence. She clutched the infant to her chest, imagining her mother's ecstasy when Lexi walked through the door in mere moments.

The side hatch opened onto the narrow street. Lexi was about to jump down when a hand shot out from behind and grasped her shoulder. Turning, she saw Raz, his nose scrunched up with distaste as he peered down at her. He moved to the rear of the spacious rover and removed a cycomp from a charging dock. He rejoined her by the open hatch and gave her a tight nod.

Lexi stepped down from the rover, followed closely by the enforcer and Raz. Outside the domicile's door, Lexi awkwardly held her brother against her shoulder as she pressed the thumb of her right hand firmly against the sensor. The door slid open, and Lexi shivered involuntarily at the sound.

Laria was seated on the edge of her bed, her shoulders slumped uncharacteristically. When Lexi and the two men stepped into the room, her mother's head snapped up and her back straightened. Laria's eyes flitted from the crying baby to the two men flanking her daughter, and all color drained from her face.

Immediately the enforcer began searching the domicile, looking through the closet and cabinets. As the helmeted man scanned their family's personal cycomp, Raz stepped around Lexi, his eyes glued to his own cycomp. "Laria, nuli worker of number 4018?"

Lexi watched as her mother got shakily to her feet and faced Raz. "Ye—" The word stuck in Laria's throat, and she coughed to clear the sound of her fear. "Yes, sir."

"Our records show you have been off the field for six months. You submitted for sick leave and were approved, it seems," the man drawled as he ran his finger down his cycomp. Lexi couldn't help but watch the shining symbols on either side of his neck move as he spoke. "Your daughter has also informed me that you recently lost a baby and are still producing milk. Is that correct?"

Lexi stared up at her mother, waiting for her to respond. But Laria's expression was one of terror, and her legs shook beneath her tunic. Lexi moved to her side, and pulled her down onto the bed with one hand. She looked into her mother's eyes, trying as hard as she could to communicate that everything was going to be okay—that these men weren't there to arrest them or harm the baby. But Laria only frowned back in confusion.

Finally Raz looked up from the screen in his hands, awaiting a response. Laria met his gaze and nodded. "That's correct, sir," she said, her voice sounding thin.

The enforcer came to stand behind Raz after finishing his search of the domicile. Raz, ignoring the towering man just behind him, looked Laria up and down with his eyebrows knit together and his lips pursed.

"You and your family will be relocated to the emperor's palace in Parahitus," he said, his voice still disinterested and businesslike. "Your husband and children will all be given new positions in the city. You will serve as a nurse for this child,"—he gestured toward Lexi and the crying infant—"the son of her royal highness, Princess Seraphina Antonia Dukales. There is no need for you to bring any of your possessions, as you will be given all new clothing and accommodations."

Lexi's heart pounded rapidly as she listened to the stout court official. Looking back at her mother, Lexi saw only pure shock written across her features. Laria swallowed hard and stood once again. She bowed slightly to Raz, and Lexi could tell she had no idea how to respond to this.

Raz's attention returned to the cycomp. The room remained completely silent with the exception of the desperate wails of Lexi's baby brother. She adjusted her hold on him for what seemed like the hundredth time as they all waited for Raz to finish typing.

"We will delay no longer then," he said after a couple minutes. "The child is clearly hungry. You will board the rover and feed him promptly, nuli worker. We will be back in a few hours to relocate the rest of your family." Raz gestured for the mother and daughter to exit the domicile ahead of himself and the enforcer.

The men followed them through the doorway and into the street where the rover was already coated in a thin layer of red dust. Lexi and Laria watched as the rover's side hatch opened. Laria took a step back at the sound of the hydraulics, her face betraying how hesitant she was to board the aircraft. Lexi was quick to take her mother's forearm and lead her into the rover. The men slipped inside behind them and made fast work of launching them skyward. Through the cockpit window, Lexi watched as the thrusters erupted in the deserted street. A cloud of red dust gusted into the empty domicile just before its door slid shut.

The ever-silent enforcer unfolded a sturdy metal bench along the rover's back wall before taking a seat in the cockpit with his back to them. Laria fell onto the bench. Lexi couldn't tell if her mother was overcome with shock or else just unable to keep her balance as they flew out of the valley.

"A wet nurse?" Laria asked, keeping her voice low. Her eyes filled with tears, and a sob escaped her lips. "The emperor's daughter wants me to nurse my own baby?"

"Well she doesn't know he's yours, does she?" Lexi asked as she placed the baby in her mother's arms. Laria sat on the edge of the bench and clung tightly to her child. For just a moment, she stared in disbelief at her baby boy before resting his head in the crook of her arm to nurse.

"I guess Ben will get to live in Parahitus after all," Laria said with a sniffle. "Thank the God of All Realms. I can't believe he's here right now." She stroked the baby's cheek as he let out a shuddering sigh through his nose. Laria looked up at her daughter. "Lexi?"

"Hm?"

"Did she give him a name?" Laria asked. Lexi's parents had never let her call him by any name, and she had never understood why. But it was obvious now that her mother had known it wouldn't be her place to name her own child. It was someone else's choice.

"She named him Calder. Because she drew him from the water."

MICHAEL SNYDER

Casting Doubt
(In Four Movements)

We Are Weak, But He Is Strong

JESUS LOVED HER, that she knew, and not just because the Bible told her so. Rachel's father said the blessing before every meal, drove them all to church on Sundays, and tearfully renewed his holy vows a few times a year. Her mother's worship was secondhand, an osmotic thing, wholly dependent on the spiritual mood of the father. Although Rachel couldn't see it at the time, she understood that it must have been a lot of pressure. So when the dam finally broke, Rachel's father washed away to a new town with a new life and a new daughter. This renovated family helped plant a new church where her father could rededicate his life to Christ with regularity. Rachel would visit on holidays, primed with a low-grade enmity for the replacement wife but never quite able to sustain it. She secretly adored her stepsister, but that too felt like betrayal. At home, Rachel's real mother found solace in mindless television, boxes of red wine, and the occasional sleepover with a former boyfriend named Stanley.

Stanley would sometimes show up at the breakfast table, smelling of cigarettes and sex, munching quietly on bran flakes and reading the paper. He was mostly a stereotype—greedy-eyed, balding, with a generous paunch and prone to wearing wifebeaters and paint-splattered jeans.

51

On such mornings, Rachel would stare at the inked rendering of Christ crucified as it twitched on Stanley's shoulder and bicep. Tattoo Jesus seemed to stare back at Rachel as if he really understood. No matter how badly she wanted to leave—her mother, this man, this room, this life—Rachel stayed put, cinching her robe tightly around her and staring at the brutal image, quietly praying that the words to the song were true.

Two Robbers Flanking Jesus

THE ATM IS STILL regurgitating twenties when the cold barrel presses into your neck.

"You believe in the afterlife?" His voice is dry, addled.

The easy answer is, Yes! Of course! I was lost and now I'm found. But the details are muddled. There was Jesus—living, dying, ascending, then your own baptism at twelve. But here, now, with the metal warming on your skin, you can't be certain what you believe. Sure, you attend services, sponsor orphans, deposit the occasional twenty when the plate passes. But if you really believed, wouldn't you . . .

"Well?" The voice is ragged now, tearstained. "I need an answer."

You ease your hand behind your back and offer him the cash but not at all what he came for. He mumbles something that sounds oddly like thanks. Then he's gone before you can get a look at him.

Playing the Odds

THERE HAD BEEN better days than these, back when he was in constant orbit around this pulpit or that one, measuring his steps more than his words, demanding eye contact from strangers, daring them to look away, basking in the thrill of connecting hopeful people to a merciful God that he still couldn't quite believe in.

Reverend James Hildebrand understood a great many things. But understanding was not the same as believing. Like when his mother had left in the middle of the night. He could see that her closet was empty, could mark the days on the calendar since he'd last felt the warmth of her fingers on the short hairs of his neck, could sense the weight of her absence burrowing into his chest. The evidence was overwhelming, yet he still woke each morning blissfully ignorant, having to relearn the awful truth all over again. It had been a preacher—his mother's preacher—that stepped in and made sure that young James had rides to school and food on the weekends. Somewhere along the way he decided to try and follow in those sizable footsteps.

The thing is, James wants to believe. So he continues to travel, reading and praying, speaking and preaching, preening and pimping for Jesus, hoping that someday he too will have ears to hear. And at the end of each day he'll pour another strong drink and sidle up to the felt-green table next to the now-familiar form of Pascal pushing his chips to the middle of the table. The philosopher will nod at the preacher, who will sit staring at that lone chip in his fingers, contemplating his next move.

A Final Shot at Redemption

YOUR NERVES ARE still shot, so you sit and try to mind your own business. But it's hard to ignore the scene playing out just a few stools away. A guy claiming to be a preacher—you haven't yet caught his name—is chatting up a skinny barfly named Rachel. He's at least ten years her senior. And the things they have in common so far include a low tolerance for family, an aversion to mindless television, and an orphaned faith in Jesus. It's a familiar scene, likely playing out in countless generic dive bars in countless towns just like this one. And unless one of them gets cold feet, they will likely end up in some state of coitus before the clock strikes midnight.

You drain your glass, ignore the barkeep's raised eyebrows, and tuck a couple of twenties under your empty glass. He's midway through wishing you a happy New Year when you hear the familiar voice.

"What about you, tough guy? You believe in the afterlife?"

You spin on your stool knowing you'll finally see the face that belongs to the man at the ATM. Most of the rest is a blur.

You approach, eyes drawn to the gun shaking in the man's hands. He's shorter than you imagined, more clean-cut, more distraught. You speak quietly, testifying to all the parts of the gospel you tried so hard to believe. But then there's fresh revelation with each step—some for you to share, some to keep. The man tells you to stop, to just shut the hell up. There are tears in his voice again. But you walk on, declaring the scandalous good news, almost against your will.

There's a flash, then a few screams and increasingly trivial commotion. Someone calls 911 and someone else rips your shirt open. The reverend prays over you as the skinny barfly presses a dirty dishrag into your wound. You want to tell her to ease up, that she's hurting you, that it doesn't really matter. The gunman is still there, mumbling, Oh God, Oh Jesus, OhJesusGodinHeaven.

Somehow this seems like a story you'll all recount together, maybe even laugh about in some not-too-distant future. And then after a while, it seems like nothing at all.

The Pain of Hunger

They are insatiable and unbearable to themselves, and it is conformable to their state that they should always be unquiet, longing and desiring that thing which they have to satiety. This is the reason why such satiety cannot content them, because they (who are infinite in their being) are always desiring something finite ... *–Saint Catherine of Siena*[1]

Anorexics be bitches. *–An anorexic*

ANOREXICS, OF COURSE, are not only women. And eating disorders manifest in myriad ways. But the reality is that most people with pronounced chronic and dysfunctional relationships with food are women. And anorexia is the most well known type of these disorders, even as it continues to be poorly understood.

Then, there's this: when I talk about eating disorders—whenever I so rarely do—I discover that it is impossible to discuss the issue as a concept. It's as if I am talking about myself in the third person. This soul and body are inextricably enmeshed, one with the other. The matter of anorexia first manifest itself to me in my body. Thus, it became identified with my self in a way I cannot readily parse.

---

1   Algar Thorold, trans., *The Dialogue of the Seraphic Virgin Saint Catherine of Siena* (London: Kegan Paul, Trench, Trubner & Co., 1907), 84.

So, when I talk about eating disorders, I say "anorexics," and when I talk about anorexics, I say "women." And when I say "women," I think "me."

※

A woman becomes an anorexic through engineering. She builds a parallel moral reality which at first augments the murky moral quagmire we all must slog through. The anorexic (or at this point, the budding anorexic) has an optimistic view of life and her own potential for self-improvement. She realizes her desires would be followed blindly to her peril, so she enjoys designing rubrics to challenge herself and incentivize the behaviors she most values.

She does this for everything. Maybe she enjoys list making! The aspirational component of imagining the day to be entirely at the mercy of her (creative, even charitable) will is exhilarating. Reading a novel for an hour definitely goes on the list! So does gardening! So does making hummus from scratch! So does tennis! "Be your best self" might be the type of slogan this woman has constantly rattling around in her solar plexus, and, Lord knows, she might even be able to attain that reality, if she could just check off enough boxes.

For this reason, it is not only a concern of the physical brain and body, but anorexia is also a pronounced spiritual stumbling block.

※

The anorexic has many wonderful and admirable qualities: compassion, kindness, self-discipline, and self-denial. These characteristics are evidenced in so many ways; this is the woman who excels at making care packages for the sick and sending birthday cards to friends far away, who drops a meal off for new parents or calls to check in on a family member who has been feeling down.

She is keenly aware of how service to the body—especially

through food—nurtures and demonstrates love to the people around her. She invariably notices if a guest needs a second helping, and is first to jump to fill it. She warms a mug of cocoa for a younger sibling coming in out of the snow. Her remarkable ability to focus outward on the well-being of others can bear fruit in a Christ-like willingness to put off gratifying her own needs.

In Catholic practice, "mortification of the flesh" is a term which refers to the intentional deprivation of one's physical desires and needs (best conducted under the guidance of a spiritual director), with the aim of strengthening faithful reliance on the Holy Spirit and growing in solidarity with the sufferings of one's earthly brothers and sisters. This includes fasting, deprivation from bodily comforts, resistance to vanity (for instance, choosing to wear ugly or unfashionable clothing), and the intentional seeking out of humbling experiences. The fruit of this practice ought to be the manifestation of love through physical acts of charity and the outpouring of a kind and generous spirit.

The idea of mortification as a spiritually beneficial practice was first introduced to the church by the Apostle Paul in his letter to the Romans: "Thus, brethren, nature has no longer any claim upon us, that we should live a life of nature. If you live a life of nature, you are marked out for death; if you mortify the ways of nature through the power of the Spirit, you will have life."[2]

> ... if her affection be placed principally in the penance she has undertaken, her perfection will be impeded; she should rather place reliance on the affection of love, ... in virtue rather than in penance. Penance should be but the means to increase virtue according to the needs of

2 Rom. 8:12–13 Knox

the individual, and according to what the soul sees she
can do in the measure of her own possibility. Otherwise,
if the soul place her foundation on penance she will
contaminate her own perfection, because her penance
will not be done in the light of knowledge of herself and
… of truth …[3]

❖

How does this admirable desire to be detached from her own wants
and needs morph into a fixation with food and denial?

The nascent anorexic initially sees her life's work in feeding
others. She envisions hospitality, making meals for others, to be a
primary interest. She reads cookbooks. She watches cooking shows.
She makes meals and desserts for family and friends. One problem
she cannot seem to get around is the degree to which hospitality
tends to be reciprocated. Her mother makes her a favorite meal.
People invite her over and offer her food. She isn't sure why, but the
hospitality of others (people she cares for and respects!) disgusts her.
Gradually, her desire to cook for friends and family diminishes—
effectively quashing the problem of reciprocity.

❖

A common heresy throughout church history has been the idea that
the carnal body and its appetites are evil, and only the spiritual
self, the soul, can be glorified. This heresy, called gnosticism, can
be recognized by its contempt for the body, its needs, desires, and
compulsions.

The church has long rejected gnosticism, noting that when God
created the physical world, he saw that it was "very good." He even

----

3 Thorold, *Dialogue of Saint Catherine*, 24.

"so loved the world that he sent his only begotten Son" to take on a physical (human) nature, which he would retain for all eternity in Heaven. God uses the physical world to confer grace on Christians in the Sacraments, especially the "real food" of the Eucharist.

If asked, the anorexic would probably concede that her body is a true, inseparable part of her being. Even so, she cultivates a divided sense of self, of which her mind/will is by far the superior half.

Her body is a constant nuisance—its hunger, yes, but also the reality that it takes up physical space. She loathes the fact that she can be seen. In that sense, her flesh is a public commodity, though not, perhaps, in a sexual way; her body reminds her continually that (like it or no) what she does to herself has the capacity to affect those around her.

The loss of pounds is delightful to her because it is a kind of erasure. Maybe by reducing the physical presence of this body in the world, she can reduce its account.

> [Dear God,] melt at once the cloud of my body. The knowl-
> edge which You have given me … constrains me to long
> to abandon the heaviness of my body, and to give my life
> for the glory and praise of Your Name, for I have tasted
> and seen with the light of the intellect in Your light, the
> abyss of You–![4]

The vocabulary used to describe eating traditions and the culture surrounding food has long been rife with moral connotations. Types of eating and exercise practices, even entire categories and kinds of food, have been equated with vice or virtue, depending on the mythology of the age.

---

4 Ibid., 135.

This has been so for most of the modern era; it is a practice deeply embedded in Western culture. One need not look far to encounter, in conversation or in advertising, certain foods (and the desires of those who feel attracted to them) labeled with the moral signifiers of temptation, seduction, and badness or tawdriness. Meanwhile, health foods, gym memberships, and the "thinspo" Instagram accounts of professional nutritionists and fitness experts are equated with "goodness," health, and moral rectitude.

Over time, the anorexic's moral view of food and exercise (as it pertains to her own self) annexes larger and larger swathes of her daily interior life. No matter how much her aspirations are for health, piety, or care for others, the temptation to conflate less with "good" and more with "bad"—or to gradually opt out of enjoying and giving thanks to God for whole groups or kinds of food (or, less obviously still, self-prescribing increasingly elaborate consequences like exercise or fasting—punishments, really—whenever one's discipline has "failed")—begins to appear to be beneficial and correct thinking.

❁

Occasionally, the anorexic will try on a new rule in the guise of a game. Let's say:

"Is it possible to eat only three grams of fat per day? How hard would it be?"

. . . Surprisingly, not that hard.

"Now, let's try something more difficult!"

❁

In the secular sphere, the only defining qualities distinguishing a "correct" relationship to food from a "disorder" are the relative health of the individual's body and the perceived psychic distress of the individual in question. There is no metric for assessing an individual's spiritual well-being or plotting the long-term trajectory of a patient who appears physically healthy but seems to be legalistic in the realm of food.

For those in the church, there is recourse to the writings of Paul in scripture. While his letters to the church in Galatia were meant to counteract a different heresy, they cut to the heart of the problem many anorexics have: legalism.

> You who look to the law for your justification have cancelled your bond with Christ, you have forfeited grace. All our hope of justification lies in the spirit; it rests on our faith; once we are in Christ, [the law] means nothing, and the want of it means nothing; the faith that finds its expression in love is all that matters.[5]

Catherine of Siena, Doctor of the Church, is one notable saint whose virtues were born out of characteristically anorexic behaviors. In learning about Saint Catherine's life, the devout must pause to wonder whether her aspirations to virtue necessitated these behaviors or whether, for her, sainthood was conferred by God despite a habit of overly zealous mortification.

While most Catholics realize that the lives of the saints should never be viewed as prescriptive, the purpose of canonization is nevertheless strongly associated with providing admirable examples of holiness lived out in the world. Even accounting for the vastly different world medieval saints like Catherine lived in, the degree to which her behaviors approximate those of a modern anorexic are startling.

From the age of 16, Saint Catherine of Siena adopted strict religious fasts, including eating only vegetables and crusts of bread,

---

5 Gal. 5:4–6 Knox

restricting herself to one meal per day, limiting her intake of water, and refusing herself sleep. She joined an order that allowed her to observe her vows at home, where she spent most of each day locked in her room, often not coming out for meals. When her mother expressed concern at the severity of her fasts, especially the lack of sleep, Catherine obediently agreed to sleep alongside her mother at night. But unbeknownst to her worried parents, she placed a board under her portion of the mattress to keep her awake as she waited for them to drift to sleep. Then she would silently escape to her cell, where she prayed on her knees for the rest of the night. Catherine was well known among the people of Siena for her holy demeanor; generosity (especially to the poor); service of the sick, including those with crippling and contagious diseases like leprosy; her ecstatic veneration of the Eucharist; and her complete disinterest in her own physical comfort.

> Observing this law in this life [the saints] taste peace without any disturbance, they receive and clothe themselves in the most perfect peace, for ... they possess every good without any evil, safety without any fear, riches without any poverty, satiety without disgust, hunger without pain, light without darkness, one supreme infinite good, shared by all those who taste it truly.[6]

☀

Self-diagnosis of anorexia (and related disorders) can be difficult. An anorexic who has never been confronted with the need for treatment likely is not aware she is endangering herself, body and soul. Indeed, she believes she is doing just the opposite.

Here are some questions for her and her loved ones to consider.

---

6 Thorold, *Dialogue of Saint Catherine*, 120.

Is she able to freely and fully give thanks for her food?

Is she able to appreciate that God made nourishment satisfying and delicious for her, as well as for others?

If so, is she eating to be satisfied? Or is she tricking herself into believing she has been filled, when in fact she is still hungry?

If she offers others a second helping, does she seriously consider having a second helping herself?

Does abandoning restrictive food rules sound frightening to her?

Is she afraid of the God of abundance?

Does her relationship with food make her more or less susceptible to the love and correction of others? Is she mortifying her flesh in order to grow in love?

If other eating disorders can be characterized by a lack of control, the anorexic's self-imposed rubrics keep her feeling coolly in charge. Strict, methodical planning (and counting and recounting of calories consumed: *better add 100 just in case the soda fountain had real Coke in the Diet Coke dispenser*) is what realizes her sense of security. While she does go to great pains to adhere to familiar routines, she also finds comfort in her ability to adapt to situations which might challenge her sense of order.

Perhaps she knows there will be a meal at a friend's house later in the day. She could decide to "save" all the calories she would normally consume, just in case there is no polite way to reduce her portions. She might also jump up before her plate is empty to help clear plates and dishes.

A critical point to understand is that all this restrictive, "best self"-focused behavior has a substantial emotional payoff. Something akin to the runner's high illuminates her mind as the anorexic frees herself from attachment to everything but the needs of those around her. Oh, and the incredible feeling she gets as she denies more and more of her own needs.

Loved ones look tired—I'll do all the cleaning!

Inability to sleep is not a problem! It gives me more time for crunches.

Sitting hurts my bony ass—how about I just stand!

The yogurt is delicious! I'll savor that one taste.

☀

The anorexic has become convinced her own incarnate reality is substantially different from others'. What is licit and good for those she loves is "dangerous," "unhealthy," or "bad" for her—and she may have many elaborate explanations for why that is so.

She sees no contradiction between her own small portions and the offers of seconds she heaps on those nearest her. The needs of others are, to her mind, needs, but the same needs of her own body are subject to negotiations with her will.

Maybe this first began as a matter of health or taste—*"I don't like greasy foods"* or *"I'll have a stomachache if I eat that"*—but by now she has been so successful in her enterprise (and food has become such a nefarious enemy) that even half a plain potato will give her excruciating stomach cramps. Through a sleight of hand, she has realized the phantom illness which at first seemed only in her imagining.

Now, what others call good really does have bad effects; her moralizing has come full circle, is made real.

☀

An anorexic who fancies herself "a serious spiritual person" might entertain the idea of fasting as a means of challenging her will to newer, purer heights. Or else, she might avoid overtly abstaining from food for fear of attracting unwanted attention (as she ventures further and further into moral territory of her own design, the necessity to confound the curiosity of others or lie becomes an obvious good; *"This is what's best for me—no one else would understand!"*). Yet, the attraction is profound: going without food altogether could offer a huge emotional high, and also the ego boost of a staggering private humility. She might plot ways to dispose of uneaten food so she can pursue her fast undetected. After all, didn't Jesus say,

> "And when you fast, do not look gloomy like the hypo-crites, for they disfigure their faces that their fasting may be seen by others. Truly, I say to you, they have received their reward. But when you fast, anoint your head and wash your face, that your fasting may not be seen by others but by your Father who is in secret. And your Father who sees in secret will reward you."[7]

Any exegetical scholar will tell you this is a directive to actively hide and lie about your food restriction, you know, as long as you do it for God.

[Her experience as an anorexic may make fasting impossible for the rest of her adult life. Will she spend every Lent ruminating on her fear of relapse? Will she visit more than one priest asking for guidance on whether fasting is, for her, safe and licit? Will she ever completely alleviate the pangs that tell her, in spiritual matters, she is never—sincerely—doing enough?]

Is there a distinction between holy fasting, especially fasting which wastes the body, and the self-denial imposed by religious anorexics? How can the woman who has had a history of eating

---

7 Matt. 6:16–18 ESV

disorders approach the concept of mortification, knowing her own proclivity to harmful denial?

> In reading the lives of the [ancients], our lukewarm blood curdles at the thought of their austerities, but we remain strangely unimpressed by the essential point, namely, their determination to do God's will in all things, painful or pleasant. —*Henry Suso, German mystic of the fourteenth century, in a letter to Elsbet Sagel* [8]

Near the end of her life, Catherine of Siena subsisted only on the Eucharist. Her confessor at one point ordered her to return to eating, but she protested that her inability to take food was an "illness." Over the course of a few months, she lost the use of her legs, and finally suffered a lethal stroke. She was thirty-three.

[The author ought to consider her own age at the writing of this essay: thirty-three. Twenty years after the onset of what could be considered her pre-anorexic ideation. Could this be why she recoils when ruminating on the life of this saint? Studying a biography of Catherine is a bit like looking into a funhouse mirror, only in this case, the reflection is the "right" self—the features of the disease made wholesome, and the author's true identity (with its warped fascinations) is the distorted copy.]

> Oh! how happy are their souls when they come to the extremity of death! ... This faith they have incarnated

---

8   M. Ann Edward. Cited Caroline Walker Bynum, "Fast, Feast, and Flesh: The Religious Significance of Food to Medieval Women," *Representations* 11 (1985): 1.

in their very marrow, and with it they see their place in [Heaven].[9]

※

Some studies indicate a staggering mortality rate among anorexics over the long term, with causes of death not strictly consigned to malnutrition or the predictable consequences of refeeding. Many anorexics die at young ages from suicide. But women in recovery die at greater rates than the general population from natural causes, too. In fact, the leading cause of death in former anorexics is heart disease.

※

The anorexic in recovery does not speak much of her life before, and when she does, it is never in any detail. Quite likely she has few legitimate memories from whole years and groups of years. But, if she is truly repentant, there is also the concern that talking about the severity of her illness will appear to others as braggadocious—as if she is proud. This is because one feature of the disease is a reckless competitive streak. Weight might fluctuate dramatically over the course of a day, but a quirk of the scale is its illusion of hard numbers. Maybe her lowest weight (at sixteen) was that of a five-year-old child—God forbid she mention that quantity to any other woman in recovery. "Oh, you were so much skinnier than I was!" her friend will say.

If she is a parent, she might worry someone vulnerable—a young daughter, for instance—might take her story prescriptively. She fears others might use her story as a playbook, culling tips to aid their own foray into the abyss.

She searches the internet for new studies of the disease out of

---

9 Thorold, *Dialogue of Saint Catherine*, 108.

a blind need for insight into what seems a bleak situation with no mapped course out. Unfortunately, she cannot find longitudinal, thirty-year studies indicating quality of life, instances of relapse, and mortality for women whose experience of the illness matches hers precisely in the following parameters: symptoms, date of onset, duration, and family patterns. What is her increased cancer risk, factoring in the Equal packets she subsisted on for the better part of three months, and the amount of diet soda she consumed over ten-plus years?

And where are the studies indicating maternal experience with the disease and likelihood of anorexia in her children?

She grasps onto hopeful statistics when she can find them, but her heart (figuratively!) skips a beat when she reads that anorexics who have struggled with the disease for more than ten years are subject to a markedly higher likelihood of long-term relapse and mortality. At this point, she shrinks from reading beyond the synopsis—she would rather have her questions left unanswered, after all.

※

The question of how to discuss the past with one's children can be troubling for the woman who still finds the specter of her disease disturbingly potent. She wonders how she can be honest with her daughter (invariably she worries more about her daughter than her sons) without communicating to her the same dis-ease.

Who knows? A child might take her mother's confidences about her history with this kind of illness not as a comforting reminder of the hope for recovery, but a harbinger of a future predestined by regrettable genetics. Faced with this possibility, a mother could be forgiven for hesitating to broach the topic of her past until she has the narrative nailed down.

[The trouble is there is no narrative, not one a child could readily comprehend. She starved herself, until her heart stopped working properly. She planned her suicide. Then, she tried to kill herself by eating vengefully; "Ninety percent of anorexics die during the refeeding process," she overheard a doctor murmuring to her parents.

She will later have no luck finding this statistic in any studies. But that figure was her lodestar as, to the initial delight of her family, she veered off her own course and began eating. Her father's warnings that she was in danger of cardiac arrest, or death through electrolyte imbalance, only served to comfort her as she plunged into what had seemed the territory of chaos and utter lack of control. For more than a year she had regarded food as though it menaced her, sure it would kill her. And now, she wanted to make sure that it would kill her, soon.]

> How cruel is the soul which offers its enemy the sword with which it is killed! For our enemies have no weapons to use against [the soul], however much they want to. Only the will can commit a crime; neither devils nor any other being can force it to commit the smallest sin if it is not willing. Therefore the sinful will which submits to the temptations of the enemy is a sword which kills the soul when it is offered to the enemy by the hand of the free will. Which is more cruel, the enemy or the person who is wounded? We are the more cruel, for we agree to our own death. *—Saint Catherine of Siena*[10]

But she, like most anorexics, will survive her initial encounter with the disease. If the numbers are correct, over the next ten years, odds are she will adopt different disordered behaviors according to her needs and circumstances: fasting for long periods (but not binging!),

---

10 Sigrid Undset, *Catherine of Siena*, trans. Kate Austin-Lund (San Francisco: Ignatius Press, 2010), 298.

fasting and binging (but not purging!), fasting and binging and purging through exercise (but not throwing up!). In all likelihood, for much of this decade she will believe that the chapter of her life in which she was a person with "food issues" has ended. Also, going by the numbers (and numbers don't lie!), she will be wrong.

What might be the most perverse physical condition for a recovering anorexic to develop? Think carefully. It will not be one you have heard of. Oh, and consider that your patient is one who has never exhibited bulimic symptoms in the years of her illness. Nothing?

Did you know there is a condition which simultaneously slows the rate at which food can be digested, while loosening the muscles that prevent food from moving upwards after it has traveled down the esophagus? There is such a condition. Somehow, this syndrome makes it possible for any type and any amount of food to travel painlessly back up the esophagus ten to thirty minutes after it was swallowed, looking and tasting just as it did when it was first consumed.

Consider your patient, who believes herself to be a recovered anorexic. How surprised she will be, when, one day, she discovers she has a new problem with food!

The relapse rate of anorexics "in recovery" is startlingly high—especially accounting for the variations of the disease which many women adopt as they attempt to relearn how to eat (bulimia, binge eating, and other behaviors such as chronic compulsive exercise are all common secondary illnesses which plague those women trying to normalize their relationship to their bodies and to food). Studies vary significantly in their statistics, but all point to one harrowing conclusion: no woman who has significantly struggled with the disease can comfortably consign that fact into her irrevocable past. She will never be a "former" anorexic, though she may, God so help her, never anymore suffer a relapse.

This patient will try to approach her new sickness proactively, visiting doctors for help with the baffling issue she now has with keeping food down. The physicians, though well meaning, will be unable to ascertain the nature of her illness. Neither will they be able to understand how her history with anorexia seems so pressingly urgent to her as she seeks help. Why can't she just keep swallowing her food? (Why, indeed?) Over the course of a year, she gradually gives up on finding help, or a cure.

It is to her as if her body has turned against her from the inside, the disorder rising up like a wave to engulf her, and she is carried off in its current.

When the anorexic transitions to bulimia, she does so with seamless elision. Somehow, even after a decade in and out of therapy, her desperate fear of food abides. What enters her mouth becomes evil to her, as though she taints food merely by touching it.

The experience of the anorexic bears similarities to that of the bulimic in a number of key ways:
- Her profound sense of isolation, even as she is keenly aware of the public aspect of her illness (her pretense of health is made sham by the barest scrutiny);
- Her keen appraisal of both her body's frail vulnerability and, paradoxically, its incredible tenacity despite compromised circumstances;

71

- She spends much of her energy each day trying to avoid encounters with food;
- Hunger;
- Shame, which makes close relationships difficult.

But there are some differences:
- As a bulimic, she spends all her money on food;
- She spends much of her time locating and assessing public bathrooms along the following criteria: proximity to food, privacy, cleanliness, and water pressure;
- Her weight stays constant;
- She longs for sleep, as it is the only rest she can find from the constant need to binge (as an anorexic, she avoided sleep almost totally);
- She discovers she is actually afraid to die.

The soul cannot live without love, but always wants to love something, because she is made of love, and, by love, [God] created her. And therefore ... the affection moved the intellect, saying, as it were, 'I will love, because the food on which I feed is love.'[11]

Rituals of food and table, of food and faith, can be a lifeline for the woman who has become habitualized to the total rejection of nourishment. She can accept that "keeping" food, by denying the compulsion to purge, is a tangible way of demonstrating love to others who care about her.

Maybe she sees this first at the altar at church, or maybe it is at the table of a welcoming family who adopts her as one of its own.

11 Thorold, *Dialogue of Saint Catherine*, 56.

Little difference; the Eucharist is a rite of adoption, and as she wit-
nesses the communion at table, she begins to know how far she has
separated herself from the brotherhood of man. Does she remember,
did she ever know, how to be human? To eat and drink with others,
to know freedom in physical pleasures, to know joy?

> Then the intellect, feeling itself awakened by the affec-
> tion, says, as it were, 'If you will love, I will give you that
> which you can love.' And at once it arises, considering
> carefully the dignity of the soul, and the indignity into
> which she has fallen through sin.[12]

At some point, the bulimic (who has heretofore been accustomed
to purging as many as twenty times a day) feels sadness for her
condition—not pity for herself, or fear of death—but sorrow that
her actions are causing others sorrow.

The sorrow alone shows her no way out, but her desire to mirror the love of those near her, and to draw closer to Christ in the
Eucharist, can teach a new way of subjecting her perfect, inviolable
will to the deep mystery of her body.

For so long she has never entered any physical encounter, especially any encounter with food, without first weighing its benefits
or its costs. But she begins to accept that there are weightier virtues
which direct the actions of others—that the selfless love of those
nearest her is somehow compelled by a strange and piercing joy.

> In the dignity of her being [the intellect] tastes [God's]
> inestimable goodness, and the increate charity with
> which [he] created her, and, in contemplating her mis-
> ery, it discovers and tastes [God's] mercy, and sees how,

---

12 Ibid.

through mercy, [he has] lent her time and drawn her out of darkness.[13]

Reconciliation is the sacrament which enables her to confess her deep shame and her utter hopelessness of recovery. It is where, for the first time (and with such wretchedness that her nose starts bleeding like a faucet, drenching her clothes), she understands that nothing in the way she understood her body or nourishment was correct, her entire moral code was upside down: what she needed was to start over again like an infant, opening her mouth and accepting what was placed there. Holding her nose to hear the absolution from the mouth of the priest, she says the prayer on the paper in her hand. The bright drops run down her fingers, blotching the page. This is how she begins teaching her will to perform the rite of gratitude.

When she accepts that food is one expression to her of God's generous love, her need to binge lessens.

Over time, she learns how to reswallow the food that her body sends back up (and to swallow, even, her own disgust). Eventually, the muscle covering her esophagus tightens somewhat. She will discover how to eat in moderation, and with gratitude. All of this will be experienced by her, not as a feat of will, but as miracle, a holy grace.

One day, (if she lives so long!) she will learn to pray to Saint Catherine, her enemy, her sister, in faith.

> It is true that suffering is over and ended, as I have said to you, for the soul that desires Me possesses Me in very truth, without any fear of ever losing that which she has so long desired; but, in this way, hunger is kept up, because those who are hungry are satisfied, and as soon as they are satisfied hunger again; in this way their satiety is without disgust, and their hunger without

---

13 Ibid.

suffering, for, in Me, no perfection is wanting.... Thus is your desire infinite, otherwise it would be worth nothing, nor would any virtue of yours have any life if you served Me with anything finite. For I, who am the Infinite God, wish to be served by you with infinite service, and the only infinite thing you possess is the affection and desire of your souls.[14]

---

14 Ibid., 82.

SAM BROUGHER

Soul-Full

ONCE THERE WAS a poor middle-aged man whose wife became pregnant. The doctors had said years ago that she was infertile, so the man and his wife became very excited. They did everything they were supposed to (prenatal checkups, etc.). The father, who was a doll designer, began sewing together a special doll for his future child.

Instead of designing the doll for manufacturing, or even using a sewing machine to speed up the process, the father spent weeks in his basement, cutting the fabric with scissors and sewing the doll by hand. The father hadn't cut or sewn by hand in decades, so one of the doll's arms was slightly bigger than the other, the legs were a little lumpy, and the smile went farther up one side of the doll's face than the other. The father was still a very skilled doll maker; only a close look could see these differences. When he finished, he left the doll bald so he could see if his child was a boy or a girl. Then, he could match the length of the doll's hair.

The father finished the doll late one night about a month before his wife was due to give birth. The last step had been to sew eyes on the doll, which he did very carefully. The doll had very realistic eyes, with blue irises, and even eyelids and eyelashes. His wife was already asleep, and he stayed up a little longer to admire his handiwork. The small imperfections in the doll, instead of making him upset, made him think the doll had character of its own (not like the mass-produced dolls he designed at work). He smiled, thinking of his future son or daughter, turned off his desk lamp, and started up the basement steps.

Thinking of the happy family he was building, he heard his wife scream in the bedroom above. The man rushed to his wife's side and immediately called an ambulance. They arrived at the hospital in minutes, but the doctors still said there wasn't anything they could do; an unforeseeable complication of the pregnancy took the father's wife and unborn child that night.

☀

For several weeks, the father did not go to work and drank too much every day. He talked to the doll he'd made as if it were his child. Sometimes, when he was very drunk, it even talked back.

His coworkers worried about him, and one eventually went to the man's house to check on him. What a sorry state the father was in by this time! He hadn't shaved since his wife died, or even bathed, nor cleaned the house at all. He left his home only to buy more booze, and the cashier assumed he was homeless.

Pizza boxes and Chinese takeout cartons sat on every available surface, often stacked several high, and most had food still in them; indeed, some hadn't been eaten from at all. Empty bottles of beer and liquor were interspersed among the boxes like giraffes poking their heads out of very small zoo cages. The combination of smells—old food, beer, sweat, and the musty smell of vermin—was almost too much for the coworker to enter the house. She took a moment to strengthen her resolve, then stepped in to talk with the father.

The father designed dolls, and this coworker designed the process to mass-produce those dolls. They had worked closely together for many years, though they rarely saw each other outside of the office.

This coworker tried to console the father, but he only cried more. She then reasoned with the father, saying that cleaning himself up and going to work would help with the pain, which only made the father cry harder. Finally, the coworker tried to cajole the father by saying his wife would be ashamed if she saw him and would want him to carry on with his life, and this made the father cry hardest of all. Finally, the coworker handed him the business card of a psychic and said, "Maybe she can help you find peace. She helped me when my father died." Then she left the father to his tears and liquor.

The father didn't say anything the entire time, only cried and drank, and he continued to drink until he passed out after the coworker left. When he woke the next morning, he was holding the doll in one hand and the psychic's business card in the other. Through bleary eyes, the father read the tagline of the business card:

I Help YOU Contact Those You LOVE In The Afterlife

The father thought about it as much as he could through his crushing hangover and decided to see the psychic. He took several hours to clean himself up; he wanted to be presentable to his wife and child if the psychic really could call them from the afterlife.

Shaving his beard took the longest time. His hand shook from the hangover, and he had to take many breaks for fear of cutting himself. While he was still half shaved, he even walked to the nearest store and bought some coffee. When he finally finished, there was so much hair it clogged his sink, and he had to pull it out and throw it in the trash.

When he was finally clean, he dressed in his best suit, which was quite threadbare. On a whim, he put the doll in his briefcase, which he took with him.

The father drove to the address on the business card, which was a small shopfront in a strip mall sandwiched between a hair salon and a pet store. The man walked in and the woman, who fulfilled all the father's stereotypes for how an aging psychic should look, immediately said, "I've been waiting for you, and so have your wife and child." The father took this as a profoundly psychic statement, not knowing that the coworker had stopped by the previous day to get the business card and told the psychic the father's story. In fact, not an hour previous the psychic had said the same thing to another man who walked in, and that man laughed and walked out immediately, since he had never been married and never had children.

The psychic charged the father a hundred dollars up front, then they went through a bead curtain into the back room. The walls of this room were painted dark blue, and most of the surface area was covered in strange white symbols, some of which appeared to be arranged together as if in sentences. The only light emanated from a hanging lamp holding several candles above the only table in the room. The flickering light reflected off the glass ball in the center of the table, giving the ball a shimmering, almost glowing, quality.

They sat down at the table and held hands. The psychic gave an exaggerated performance of calling the souls, even though, really, the souls were eager to come and needed little coaxing. First, the father and his wife talked, and this communication the psychic conducted faithfully. How happy the man was to hear his wife was happy in Heaven, for she was faithful and repentant in life. He cried still, but this time with smiling eyes and a lighter heart.

Unfortunately for the father, the psychic was behind on her bills, and greedy besides. When the father spoke to his child, the psychic did not faithfully transmit what the child said. Instead of saying how happy the daughter was in Heaven, and how she didn't have any cares or worries, and how she was looking forward to seeing her father in Heaven in good time, the psychic said that a demon had taken hold of his daughter's soul and was tormenting her.

This greatly distressed the father, and he immediately asked what could be done. The psychic licked her lips, dry from lying. She said they could pull the daughter out of the demon's grasp and put her soul in some vessel in the world, something made by man, such as a picture. Only this could free her soul from the demon's grasp. "But it will be very expensive," the psychic said, "because of the great risk I will be taking in angering the demon."

This made the soul of the mother very angry, and she struck the psychic in the face. The psychic cried out, and a bruise developed quickly on her cheek. She said the demon was angry with her proposal to rescue the child's soul. The father, in shock, immediately agreed to pay the psychic a large sum of money every month for five years, for the psychic would only be able to keep the daughter's soul on Earth for that length of time.

The psychic asked where the daughter's soul should be placed, and the father retrieved the doll from his briefcase and set it on the table. This pleased the psychic greatly. The closer to human the soul vessel, the safer and easier the psychic could get the soul into it. She immediately set about placing the daughter's soul into the doll.

The mother became worried now, and she tried to talk directly to the father, telling him to stop the psychic, but the father was not listening. The frustrated mother blew out the candles so the only light in the room filtered through the bead curtain from the other room. This did not disturb the psychic at all and only strengthened the resolve of the father. The mother attacked the psychic again, scratching at her arms and trying to rip the doll out of her hands, but, though the psychic gasped in pain, she would not release the doll, and continued to force the daughter's soul into it. When the father saw the wounds appear on the psychic's arms, he yelled, "Begone, demon!" The mother began to cry, kissed her husband lightly on the cheek, and faded back to Heaven. She and God had an argument, but, of course, God had a Plan, and, once the mother understood the Plan and trusted in God, she was happy and worry free once again.

At this point, the psychic succeeded in placing the soul of the child into the doll, and the doll blinked her blue thread eyes and came to life. The psychic had erased the soul's memories of Heaven, so when the father asked what she remembered, all the doll mentioned was darkness, yelling, and pain, her last memories in her mother's womb in the hospital just before she died. The father, pleased to have

81

"saved" his daughter, gladly wrote the psychic a check for a thousand dollars, which was most of his savings.

As he stepped into the parking lot, the father stopped, startled, and stared at the doll in his hands. "A daughter! You were my daughter the whole time!"

☀

The father, now in good spirits, cleaned up the house for his daughter, set the nursery to rights, and began to go to work again. His coworkers marveled at the sudden change, but he kept the reason secret from them. The doll was happy with her father, and she amused herself with the many toys the father bought her.

Several weeks passed, and the doll became bored, even with all her toys, because she was not allowed to leave the house. The father said that other people wouldn't understand a moving doll, but she promised not to move when they went out, so the father took her to see a movie in the theater. Other people looked strangely at the father, since he held the doll as one would a child, but he didn't mind and the doll was pleased to be able to see the outside world.

During the movie, a kids' film with talking animals, they sat behind a mother with two children. This woman had long blond hair, and the doll greatly admired it. In fact, the doll didn't watch the movie at all, but instead admired this woman's hair, and how the hair shone in the light from the movie. The doll felt her bald head, and decided that she would take the hair for herself. She grabbed a tiny fistful of the hair and yanked, but was unable to pull the hair out. The woman yelped in pain, turned around and yelled at the father, then found a security guard. The father said that his keys had gotten stuck in her hair, but the woman and the guard didn't believe him and he was thrown out of the movie theater and told never to return.

The father asked the doll why she had pulled the woman's hair, and the doll said she thought the hair was so pretty that she had to have it for her own. This worried the father, and he told her she couldn't just take other people's hair. The doll started crying and asked why she couldn't, and the father explained how this was painful for people, and how you can't take things that belong to other people without asking, but the doll didn't understand or care about any of this and continued to cry because she couldn't have the beautiful hair she wanted.

"I don't have any hair at all!" the doll cried. "I'm so ugly!"

The father sighed, exasperated. "We can get you some hair. Just don't take someone else's hair."

He asked her what type of hair she would like. The doll thought for a minute, then said she wanted hair like his, but long like the woman in the theater. So the father went to a craft store and found some yarn that was the same brown color as his hair, and set about making the doll some hair. When the doll saw the yarn, she saddened once again because yarn is not like actual hair, not even a little. So the father discarded the yarn and cut off most of his own hair, which he then meticulously, strand by strand, sewed into the doll's head. This took many evenings, but afterward the daughter was pleased with her new hair.

After several days, the doll's mood slowly soured again. She had real hair, true, but it was short, not like the long, long hair of the woman in the theater. Eventually, in the face of many tantrums, the father went out and asked women if he could cut off and keep their hair if he gave them some money. After several nos, numerous strange looks, and one threat to call the police, he convinced a hair salon to give him a bundle of blond trimmings, and he brought the hair home to the doll.

The doll was overjoyed! She immediately braided and tied the hair into her own, and she now had hair down to her feet! For hours she stood in front of the mirror and admired her new hair, often spinning in circles so her hair would twirl like a skirt. Since the doll was pleased, so was the father. The father would take the daughter out to the park or the movies, and they were both content for a long while.

At work, the father had even been caught whistling merrily. The coworker commented on the father's changed mood. "I haven't seen you this happy since . . ."

"I must thank you and your psychic for that," the father replied. "She has given me only a reprieve from my sadness, I'm afraid, but a much-welcomed one. Who knows? Maybe we can make it permanent."

Startled, the coworker asked what the father could possibly mean and what the psychic had done for him. The coworker only thought the psychic could contact the dead, and even then maybe as a charlatan's trick. She did not even suspect the psychic's other powers, so the father wasn't making sense to her. But the father only smiled and nodded and deflected the coworker's further questions.

☀

Alas, the doll was not content for as long as the father had hoped. She saw someone whose hair she liked more than her own, and she wanted that hair as well. She asked her father, who said she had enough hair and should be happy with it. This upset the doll, and she started to cry again. The father tried to comfort her, because he knew he couldn't afford to keep buying people's hair. And, anyway, he thought teaching her to be content with what she had was important. But the doll would not be consoled.

One night, while the father was asleep, the doll decided to find new hair on her own. She sneaked out of an open window and into a neighbor's house. A woman and her husband lived there, along with their two children, a boy and a young girl. The woman was not very attractive, and she didn't have the best-kept hair, but it was bright red and unlike any hair the doll had seen. She found a pair of scissors and carefully cut off most of the woman's hair, as well as most of the daughter's hair, which was also red but not as bright, and sneaked back to her father's house. She carefully wove and braided the hair into the hair on her head and was very pleased with the results, especially how the red hair contrasted with the brown and blond hair already on her head.

When the father woke, the doll excitedly showed off her new hair. The father, angered, interrogated her, asking where she got the hair. The doll sulked, the fun of having new hair ruined, and refused to tell him. Nevertheless, when the police arrived at the neighbor's house, the father suspected, correctly, that she had stolen the hair from them. When the police came to his door and asked him if he saw anything, he said that he'd slept soundly the entire night, sorry.

Once the police left, the father, very angry with the doll, yelled at her and confined her to her room. The doll became angry and yelled back, saying she was her own person and could make her own decisions. The father responded by saying she wasn't allowed to make her own decisions. After that, the doll sulked more and wouldn't talk to the father. This lasted for several days, during which time the father was very careful to secure all the windows and doors whenever he left so the doll couldn't sneak out.

Eventually, the doll became dissatisfied with her hair again and wanted more, but the father decided that the doll absolutely must learn to appreciate what she had, particularly since she'd go to such lengths to get more. He refused. Since the doll couldn't leave the house and get some on her own, he reasoned, over time she must accept what she had. The doll despaired and stopped talking to the father entirely, spending most of her time arranging and rearranging, braiding and unbraiding her hair.

One night, the father woke and found himself tied to his bed. There was a strange weight on him, and from the light of the streetlamp outside he could see the doll was standing on his chest, a shaving razor in her hand. He asked what she was doing, but the doll only responded by muttering, "More hair," and set to work shaving the hair off the father. She wasn't very skilled at shaving, and she wasn't very careful, so she cut the father many, many times. Each time she cut him, the father gasped in pain, but she did not notice. She took not just the hair from his head but also the shorter hairs from his arms, legs, and chest, weaving all of these hairs, as best she could, into the hair already on her head. Then she took a pair of scissors, used them to break a hole in the bedroom window, and jumped out, leaving her father behind.

Eventually, the father worked his way free from the rope tying him to the bed. He searched for the doll but couldn't find her anywhere. He was sad that she had run away, scared of what might happen to her, and worried that she would continue stealing hair, particularly since she didn't even care if she hurt her own father. He stopped going to work again and spent all his time looking for the doll. He started in the immediate area around his home, searching through bushes, yards, and alleys, spiraling outward as he went, all without luck.

After several days, he saw a story in the newspaper headlined, "The Puppet Shaver." The article detailed how two different women on consecutive nights had been tied down in the middle of the night and completely shaved. Both women lived alone and had previously had long, straight hair. All either person saw of their attacker was a small female doll, which they thought was a puppet. One had received several superficial cuts during the process, but the second one had not been injured at all.

That very day, the father needed to make his monthly payment to the psychic. The father decided that, while he was there, he would ask the psychic for help, and he returned to her shop in the strip mall.

The psychic, annoyed at the man's request, wouldn't help him without another even larger payment! The father refused, because he didn't have the money, and he was already paying her so much he thought she should help him. He threatened to not pay the rest of what he owed her if she did not help. This angered the psychic and she brought forth an evil soul. The soul threw the father into the back room then held him by the throat on the table with the glass ball.

"Fool!" the psychic cackled at him. "You can't threaten me! You will continue to pay me what I ask, or I will bring your wife out of Heaven so that her soul will rot on Earth just as I have your daughter!"

The father, panicking, grabbed the psychic's glass ball and threw it at her. It struck her in the head and broke. The psychic lost control of the evil soul, which leaped into a nearby samurai figurine and ran out the door. The father held down the psychic, and she broke down, apologizing and begging. She said her debts were out of control, and not enough people believed in psychics to sustain her business. She confessed to pulling his daughter's soul out of Heaven, not the grip of a demon.

"If a soul remains on Earth for too long in an idol, it will rot and fade away into nothingness," the psychic said. "It will go to neither Heaven nor Hell, just oblivion. If the soul's vessel is destroyed, the soul will return to where it came from."

The father demanded she help him find the doll, but she couldn't without the glass ball to focus her energy.

☼

The father returned home and found the addresses of the attacks and determined what general direction the doll was headed. Every night he went looking for her, and every night he failed to find her. As new attacks occurred, he plotted the doll's direction on his map.

One night, while out searching, the father heard a scraping sound like a rug being dragged across the ground. He chased the sound and barely saw a woven mat slide in the partially opened window of a house. He carefully opened the window farther and crawled inside, landing with a loud *thump!* on the hardwood floor of someone's living room.

The smell hit him like diving into water: body odor, wet dog, and rotting fruit. The woven mat was longer than the father was tall and about half as wide. It lay completely flat on the ground except for a lump at the opposite end from the father. The mat crept silently away from him toward a doorway. The father quickly grabbed the end of the mat and tugged. The lump on the other side hissed and turned, revealing the doll, who narrowed her eyes at the father and leaped onto a nearby couch. She shoved a floor lamp toward the father, who dropped the doll's woven hair to catch the lamp. The doll flitted away toward the window, fast despite the amount of hair dragging behind her. Just before leaping out the window, she turned back to the father and pushed over a small lamp on an end table. The father was too far away to catch the lamp, and it shattered on the floor. Someone yelled from deeper in the house, and the father scrambled out the window after the doll.

He picked a direction and ran. Luck—or something else, perhaps—was on his side, and he heard skittering the next yard off. He scrambled awkwardly over a fence, caught sight of the hair rug moving into an alley, and raced after it.

The doll ran onto a bridge over a river, lighted by small lamps. She whirled around just before the father reached her again.

"You can't stop me," the doll hissed. "I need it! Don't you under-stand?" She sulked. "I'm a freak without it. But I can be beautiful."

"It's time to go home, now," the father said sternly, approach-ing slowly with his hands making calming motions in front of him. "Surely you have enough hair. And look at the state your hair's in." On the lighted bridge, the father could clearly see that the mat of hair was encrusted with filth; mushrooms studded it like barnacles. "It definitely needs to be washed and rebraided. Don't you see? You need to come home with me, and we can take care of everything."

"No!" the doll shouted, pulling a straight razor out of her clothes. "You'll never trap me again!"

The father reached forward, grabbed the doll, and picked her up. The doll screamed and slashed at him with the razor, cutting sharply across his left wrist. He dropped her in pain and surprise. Now on the ground, the doll rushed forward and hacked at his leg, but couldn't get a good cut through his pants. The father, by reflex, kicked at the doll, and she tumbled off the bridge, taking her hair with her.

The hair rug, doll attached, floated almost lazily through the air before slapping into the river below.

"Next time I'll kill you!" the doll shouted at the father as she drifted beneath the bridge. "Just leave me alone!"

The father let out a shuddering breath and wrapped his injured arm in the bottom of his shirt. He thought about what the psychic had said. The soul will rot and fade away . . .

Sirens approached, and before the father got off the bridge a police car sped past him going the other direction. The father pretended to be out for a walk, his arms crossed against the night chill. His heart beat in his ears like a drum.

At home, the father carefully wrapped a bandage around his wrist. The wound was serious enough that he should get stitches, but he didn't want to answer any difficult questions.

The father couldn't find the doll again before her next attack. This time, instead of the generally straight direction the doll previously went, the attack occurred on the completely opposite side of the city. The father didn't know what pattern the doll was following now, or how she managed to move the many miles from one side of the city to the other. After several more attacks, no patterns emerged. The doll stayed in the city, but she attacked seemingly random places across the city's length and breadth.

☀

As time went on, the public feared the Puppet Shaver more and more. The police continued to have no leads, because they looked, incorrectly, for a person. The attacks now occurred at regular intervals, an attack almost every week. The victims were always women, always had straight, long hair, and always lived alone. Almost all the women were wealthy enough to own or rent a house by themselves, but occasionally an apartment was broken into.

The father better organized his plotting of the attacks. He bought a wall-sized map of the city and put pushpins in the map. He connected the pins with string in the order the attacks occurred. The map began to look more and more like tentacles stretched out from the center of the city. Thinking the doll couldn't possibly be moving so far on foot, the father decided she must be hitching rides without people noticing.

One day while the father stared at the map of attacks, his boss knocked on the door to his house. They'd always gotten along well, but the boss increasingly worried over the father not showing up for work. The father explained, somewhat, how he had to work through some personal stuff. The boss told him that he was trying to be understanding but was supposed to fire the father. The boss was a kind man, however, and gave the father another week to return.

As he was leaving, the boss saw the map and said, "Why are you mapping out the bus routes?" The father said that it was part of the personal stuff he needed to finish. He ushered the boss out of the house, checked the location of the downtown bus transfer station, then quickly drove there.

Buses came and went, but the father never saw the doll. People stepped on and off the buses. He talked to some, pretending his daughter had lost a doll on the bus, and then he talked to the bus drivers about a lost doll, but no one had seen anything. At the end of the day, the buses stopped running and the father went home, worried because an attack hadn't occurred in several days.

He went back the next day and sneaked into the maintenance area for the buses. He searched as thoroughly as he could without being seen all day and into the night, but still he did not find the doll. When the last buses were leaving the station, he faintly heard a scraping sound on the asphalt. He rushed to the buses and saw the doll's woven hair disappear under the last bus. The bus began to pull away, so he ran to the door and waved at the driver, who stopped and let him on.

The father stood in the middle of the bus and watched carefully out the windows for the doll. People slowly filtered on and off the bus until only he and a blond woman with straight hair were left. Just the type of hair the doll liked. The driver pulled the bus over.

The woman left the bus, and the driver said, "This is the last stop, buddy. After this we head back downtown. You gettin' off?" The father started to say, no, he was fine going back downtown, but out of the corner of his eye he saw the doll's hair scurrying after the woman, so he thanked the driver and rushed after them.

The woman walked into a rundown apartment building in a rundown neighborhood. The doll followed but went around to the side of the building. When the father turned the corner to the alley behind the apartment building, the doll was gone. Two men, apparently homeless, were warming themselves over a metal barrel with a fire in it. The father was just about to ask if either of them had seen a doll with a rug attached to its head wandering around on its own when he heard a sliding, slithering sound above him. Looking up, he saw the doll scampering up the fire escape.

The father climbed onto a dumpster under the fire escape and leaped to the ladder. When he grabbed it, his weight pulled the sliding ladder down, but it creaked to a halt after only a foot. The doll, hearing the sound, looked down at him, then scampered faster up the fire escape. The father slowly pulled his arms up and put his elbows through the ladder. Eventually, he was able to pull himself onto the lowest level of the fire escape. Gasping for air, he stumbled to his feet and rushed up the fire escape stairs. He couldn't see the doll. As he went, the father checked to make sure the windows were closed along the fire escape. He eventually reached the roof.

Poised stiffly in the middle of the roof, the doll glared at him with her tiny arms crossed. She had detached her mass of hair, leaving only her father's hair sewn carefully into her head.

"Why do you hate me, Daddy?"

The question stopped the father briefly. He remained silent and slowly approached his daughter.

"I need the hair!" she shrieked, then whispered, "How else can I be a pretty little girl?"

The father remained silent and continued to approach the doll. "It's time to go home," the father said, stopping a few feet short of her.

"You'll just lock me up again in that stupid house and I never get any new hair."

"No I won't," the father said, shaking his head, tears falling from his eyes. "It's time to go back to your mother."

"Mommy?" The doll's eyes widened. "You said Mommy's . . ." She took several steps back onto her hair. "You—you're going to kill me? You're going to kill your daughter?"

"I'm taking you home now," the father whispered, then dove forward and tackled the doll onto the rug of hair.

The doll screamed in fear, and the father grabbed the edges of the hair mat and pulled them together, creating a sack with the doll trapped inside. He wrapped the hair around itself as much as he could to trap her, gagging on the smell of rot as his hands squished into the mat. He sprinted back to the fire escape.

The doll yelled and struggled in the bundle of hair, trying to fight her way to the surface. She sliced through layers of hair with her straight razor, lost it, then tore through with her hands. She got an arm out, which she used to feebly strike the father's hand and forearm.

The father was mostly down the fire escape when her other arm came out the same hole as the first and forced it open farther. The father reached the last level of the fire escape when the doll's head emerged from the bundle, furious at being trapped. The father judged the distance to the burning barrel of the homeless men and choked as he said, "Goodbye, my love. Give your mother a kiss for me." He grabbed the doll by the head and tossed her into the barrel. The doll screamed wordlessly in anger and fear, at first, then screeched as her vessel was destroyed.

Then her soul departed.

The mass of hair and muck weighed a ton in the father's hands. He dropped it to splat wetly onto the floor of the fire escape. The father yelled and slammed his foot into it, over and over again. He stomped and kicked the hair apart until most of it had fallen to the ground below, and the rest clung damply to the metal grate of the fire escape.

He stopped, breathing heavily, and saw a glint of metal in the remaining mess. He bent over and picked up the straight razor. Opened it, wiped the blade on his pants to clean it.

The edge of the blade glowed red from the fire below. The father stood, arms held loosely in front of himself, and stared at the knife. Hypnotized, he swayed slightly on his feet.

"Hey! You there! Are you okay?" one of the men below yelled.

The father started out of his reverie. He carefully folded the razor and placed it in his pocket. Then he collapsed on the fire escape, sobbing.

Contributors

SAM BROUGHER, in his day job, is an educational software engineer. At night, he raises a flock of daughters with his wife and cats, and spends any spare moments he can writing fantastical fiction and open source programs at forestazuaron.com.

MARIAN JACOBS grew up in sunny Southern California, and now resides near Houston, Texas. She is a stay-at-home mom, photographer, and writer. She and her husband, Tim, have three beautiful children. You can read more from her at www.majacobs.com.

AMARIS FELAND KETCHAM is an honorary Kentucky Colonel and assistant professor at the University of New Mexico. She occupies her time with open space, white space, CMYK, flash nonfiction, long trails, f-stops, line breaks, and several Adobe programs running simultaneously. Her work has appeared in *Creative Nonfiction*, the *Los Angeles Review*, *Prairie Schooner*, *Rattle*, and the *Utne Reader*.

SARAH BEN OLSON writes poetry and non-fiction from her busy home in Eastern Washington.

MICHAEL SNYDER lives in middle Tennessee with his amazing wife and children. His work has appeared or is forthcoming in *The First Line; Relief Journal; Cease, Cows; Foliate Oak; Everyday Fiction; Lit.Cat; Cicatrix Publishing,* and various other online haunts. His first three novels were published by HarperCollins/ Zondervan. Michael earned a degree in music Composition and Arranging from Belmont University and can often be found coaxing sound out of stringed instruments, sometimes in a band called Elvis Shrugged. (michaelsnyderwrites. wordpress.com)

Colophon

Body text is set in Nimbus Roman No9. Block quotes, copy-right information, and running heads are set in Palanquin, with story titles in **Palanquin Dark**. **Roboto Slab** is used on the title and half-title pages and in some headings.

AW CONQUEROR is displayed on the cover.

Greater Sum is printed in the United States on a 60 lb. natural paper stock.

The first issue of *Greater Sum* debuted at the West Coast Christian Writers Conference in February 2017.

Submission Information

Greater Sum is a journal of prose and faith. This is meant to be interpreted broadly, with the art and the spirit guiding the submission and selection process. We accept fiction and narrative nonfiction and encourage essays, especially experimental forms.

We encourage work by people of faith or that has faith as its subject—it need not be both and the connection need not be overt.

There is no reading fee for submissions.

Full guidelines: **www.agreatersum.com/submit**

Subscription Information

Greater Sum publishes twice annually, in spring and fall. Pricing:
Single issue: $7
One-year subscription (2 issues): $13
Two-year subscription (4 issues): $25
If you are purchasing for a religious organization, school, or non-profit, or would like to purchase 10 or more copies, please email **subscribe@agreatersum.com** to inquire about special pricing.

Subscribe online: **www.agreatersum.com/subscribe**

And whatever you do, do it heartily, as to the Lord and not to men.

www.ingramcontent.com/pod-product-compliance
Lightning Source LLC
Chambersburg PA
CBHW030603130626
46552CB00006B/2647